A.S.K.

A.S.K.

Ask

Seek

Knock

CRAIG R. PLANTS

Copyright © 2024 Craig R. Plants

All rights reserved.
No portion of this book may be reproduced – mechanically, electronically, or by any other means, including photocopying - without written permission of the author.
Contact the author: crp708@gmail.com

Scripture quotations taken from the 21st Century King James Version®, copyright © 1994. Deuel Enterprises, Inc., Gary, SD 57237. All rights reserved.

ISBN-13: 979-8-9915961-0-7

⁹ But as it is written: "Eye hath not seen, nor ear heard, neither have entered into the heart of man the things which God hath prepared for them that love Him."

¹⁰ But God hath revealed them unto us by His Spirit. For the Spirit searcheth all things, yea, the deep things of God.

¹¹ For what man knoweth the things of a man, save the spirit of man which is in him? Even so no man knoweth the things of God, but the Spirit of God.

¹² Now we have received, not the spirit of the world, but the Spirit which is of God, that we might know the things that are freely given to us by God.

¹³ These things also we speak, not in the words which man's wisdom teacheth, but which the Holy Ghost teacheth, comparing spiritual things with spiritual.

¹⁴ But the natural man receiveth not the things of the Spirit of God, for they are foolishness unto him; neither can he know them, because they are spiritually discerned.

¹⁵ But he that is spiritual judgeth all things, yet he himself is judged by no man.

I Corinthians 2:9-15

A.S.K.

Table of Contents

Introduction	vii
Foundations	4
According to God's Will	18
Seek & Knock	37
Decisions	60
Big Prayers	92
Pray for One Another	103
Health	115
Shhh…it's a secret	127
Epilogue	131

A.S.K.

Introduction

Ask, and it shall be given you; seek, and ye shall find; knock, and it shall be opened unto you: For every one that asketh receiveth; and he that seeketh findeth; and to him that knocketh it shall be opened. (Matthew 7:7-8)

As I sat down to write, I imagined you had taken a seat with me and asked about prayer. My response would begin a long conversation, as I have much to share. The problem is that nobody ever asks. I suspect the contents will surprise my friends and family, and they will inquire, "Why did you never tell me these things?" My response will be, "Because you never asked."

In a sense, this serves as an appropriate opening. I think our relationship with God is lacking and our prayers are weak because we never ask. We aren't sufficiently inquisitive; the pursuit of God becomes neglected. We consume spiritual calories, but we rarely spend any of the spiritual energy necessary for the strenuous work of seeking God. Life in America is full of abundance and, therefore, we don't actively pursue God. There are seldom pressing needs demanding a change in our habits. Attending church once a week, or once in a while, seems good enough. The Bible often sits undisturbed. The media's constant bleating takes the place of quiet contemplation.

I wonder if, upon standing before God, we will discover many truths, exclaiming, "Why did I never know this?" and God responding, "Because you never asked."

1

Foundations

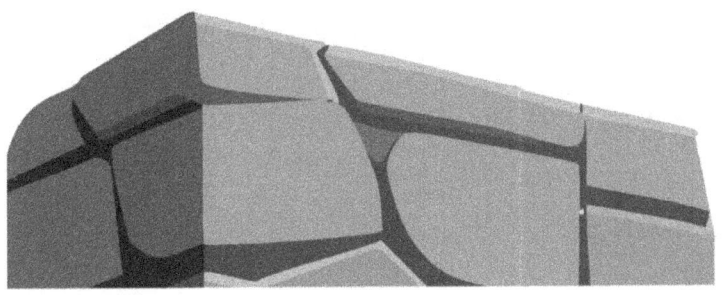

1

Foundations

"Lord, teach us to pray as John also taught his disciples." (Luke 11:1)

There was a time I did not differ from the disciples of Jesus. I didn't know how to pray. After years of futility, I followed the Bible's example and uttered a simple prayer, 'Lord, teach me to pray.'

You can find the answer to that prayer within these pages.

My understanding grew over time through personal Bible reading (loads of personal Bible reading), circumstances, and experimentation with the concepts I was uncovering within the Bible. I use the word 'experimentation' frequently because the wisdom of the Bible truly came alive once I applied it to everyday life.

If you've spent time in church, you are aware of different types of prayer; confession and acknowledging your sin for repentance; gratitude and thanksgiving; adoration and worship. These forms of prayer are necessary and important.

However, this book focuses in on prayer requests and petitions. Your requests for help can yield substantial results if you apply the Bible's principles to the process.

A.S.K.

THE COURTROOM

An analogy is the best place to begin. Let's imagine you have an important legal matter to address and the court has established a date for your appearance. This requires you to stand before the judge and plead your legal case. For most, this scenario would be intimidating.

Do you think it would be wise to arrive at the court with no preparation? To simply do your best and hope for a successful outcome? I think we would all agree that this would be foolish.

Instead, you would hire legal counsel to help prepare your case. The point is simple: you would not appear before a judge with no preparation.

The analogy is straightforward: you have a prayer request. With your prayer, you are entering a courtroom, and the judge is God. Do you think it is wise to enter God's court with no preparation?

"And I saw a great white throne and Him that sat on it, from whose face the earth and the heaven fled away, and there was found no place for them." (Revelation 20:11)

If you will, then try to imagine standing before God with a request. You can easily imagine a local courthouse room and proceedings. Now extend that concept into a spiritual courtroom setting. The Bible offers some helpful imagery.

"....a throne was set in Heaven, and One sat on the throne. And He that sat thereon was to look upon like a jasper and a sardius stone; and there was a rainbow round about the throne, in appearance like unto an emerald.
And round about the throne were four and twenty seats; and upon the seats I saw four and twenty elders sitting, clothed in white raiment, and they had on their heads crowns of gold.
And out of the throne proceeded lightnings and thunderings and voices. And there were seven lamps of fire burning before the

throne, which are the seven Spirits of God; and before the throne there was a sea of glass like unto crystal. And in the midst of the throne, and round about the throne, were four living beings full of eyes in front and behind." (Revelation 4:2-6)

The Bible depicts God as the Judge of the Earth. If you have a request, then you are not wasting your time praying to the One who has full authority to grant your request. However, approach the situation with reverence, as well as preparation according to the Judge's instructions - the Bible.

"O Lord God, to whom vengeance belongeth—O God, to whom vengeance belongeth, show Thyself. Lift up Thyself, Thou judge of the earth; render to the proud their due reward." (Psalm 94:1-2)

"Shall not the Judge of all the earth do right?" (Genesis 18:25)

"But our God is in the heavens: He hath done whatsoever He hath pleased." (Psalm 115:3)

I truly believe Psalms 115:3 is a pivotal statement. God does whatever He wants. No one can stop or resist Him. Ecclesiastes 7:13 asks, 'Who can make straight that which He has made crooked?'. If you have faith to believe this is true, then you are off to a good start.

Now that you have some Bible imagery to assist, let's go back to imagining the event of approaching God with your request. Imagine a massive door opening upon a gigantic heavenly space with an imposing throne. Do you think you should say whatever pops into your mind, or recite a few remarks prepared by another, and then hope for the best?

If you are like me, then this is how I approached prayer for decades. I was completely unprepared. I said a few words and hoped for the best. My prayers all sounded similar, 'I pray for this, I pray for that, Amen.' Eventually I tried to pray without using the word 'pray,' and it was difficult. The redundancy of using the word 'pray' repeatedly while praying is amusing, if you think about it. If you talked like this to another person, they would think something is wrong with you. There was little evidence that my prayers mattered; prayer seemed futile.

However, everything changed when I started with the simple request, 'Teach me to pray'. If you struggle with prayer, then start here. If you really want that prayer answered, read your Bible. I would suggest reading it from cover to cover at least once a year to start, and then continue to increase the pace. For me, what started as a chore eventually became a pleasure.

These two things might seem too simple—pray for guidance on how to pray and then read your Bible—but it's necessary. Prayer is not futile. Answers to your prayers are possible.

POWERFUL & EFFECTIVE

"The effectual fervent prayer of a righteous man availeth much." (James 5:16)

Look at the three concepts presented in this verse: effectual (i.e., effective), fervent, and righteous. 'Effectual' means you are successful in producing the intended result. 'Fervent' is passionate intensity. 'Righteous' means you are acting in accord with divine or moral law. If I may offer a paraphrase of the same verse: 'The passionately intensive prayer of a person acting in accordance with God's written word is both effective and powerful.'

Let's examine the entire section of scripture in its context.

"Confess your faults one to another, and pray one for another, that ye may be healed. The effectual fervent prayer of a righteous man availeth much.
Elijah was a man subject to like passions as we are. And he prayed earnestly that it might not rain, and it rained not on the earth for the space of three years and six months. And he prayed again, and the heaven gave rain and the earth brought forth her fruit." (James 5:16-18)

When I've heard James 5:16 taught, the focus was often on the 'fervent' prayer. I thought if I dedicated more time to prayer, then successful results would follow. The only hurdle between me and a successful prayer was time.

Fervent prayer is indeed important, but by itself, there is a problem. Jesus said, "But when ye pray, use not vain repetitions, as the heathen do, for they think that they shall be heard for their much speaking." (Matthew 6:7). Excessive repetition is not the answer.

Instead, shift your attention to the second part of the statement: the prayer of a 'righteous' man. This brings us to a key consideration: righteousness.

When pondering righteousness, I'm not referring to trying to earn God's salvation through good works, as the Bible states that our good works are insufficient for obtaining eternal life. Eternal life only comes through Jesus Christ. 'Jesus said unto him, "I am the Way, the Truth, and the Life; no man cometh unto the Father, but by Me." (John 14:6)

However, as Christians, we strive for righteousness through righteous living. The Bible serves as the instruction manual for righteousness, as mentioned in II Timothy.

"All Scripture is given by inspiration of God and is profitable for doctrine, for reproof, for correction, for instruction in righteousness, that the man of God may be perfect, thoroughly equipped for all good works." (II Timothy 3:16-17)

As Christians, we are to pursue righteousness. "But thou, O man of God, flee these things and follow after righteousness, godliness, faith, love, patience, meekness." (I Timothy 6:11).

Here is the simple truth: Once we become Christians, we can no longer live as we please. We are no longer our own little god, and our focus can't be on self-realization and fulfilling our desires. God commands us to repent of our sins and strive for righteousness.

A.S.K.

"The night is far spent; the day is at hand. Let us therefore cast off the works of darkness, and let us put on the armor of light. Let us walk honestly as in the day, not in rioting and drunkenness, not in lewdness and wantonness, not in strife and envying. But put ye on the Lord Jesus Christ, and make not provision for the flesh to fulfill the lusts thereof." (Romans 13:12-14)

While you can spend hours reciting prayers, if you neglect to devote time pursuing a righteous lifestyle and cultivating righteous habits (such as reading your Bible), your prayer's success rate is likely to suffer. It could even be abysmal. I refrain from saying 'will be abysmal' because I believe Psalm 115:3 and that God does whatever He wants. You might be a wicked sinner, and God might still answer your prayer. I can't predict what God will or won't do in your specific situation. All I know is that God does what He wants.

However, if you're a Christian and want to enhance your prayers and increase the likelihood of God granting your requests, then you need to focus on cultivating a righteous lifestyle. 'The prayer of a righteous man is powerful and effective.'

You see, if God is the judge and I'm entering His courtroom with my request, then I must prepare. I view this preparation as a daily practice. It's minute-by-minute and hour-by-hour. It's day-by-day as I pursue righteousness. That is my goal: to be a righteous man.

This daily preparation is crucial because I never know when I'm going to need to enter God's courtroom with my prayer request. I know life is hard. The suffering I've faced and endured happens without advanced notice. Life is full of suffering. At any moment, I risk encountering a situation that upends my life. When I run an errand, or attend a routine medical appointment, or answer the phone, everything in life might change.

In those moments, I want to be fully prepared to walk into God's courtroom with my 'solemn request for help'.

I won't wait until things are dire to ask for forgiveness; I'll seek forgiveness daily. I won't wait until the times are tough to seek God; I'll seek God daily by reading His Bible and applying His commands and guidance to my life. I won't wait for situations to spiral out of control to live righteously; I'll live righteously now.

You see, God knows you. He knows everything about you. It's unwise to postpone righteous living until the storms of life arrive. Let's be honest—there are storms of life on your horizon (if they haven't already arrived). Evading suffering is impossible. So, don't postpone righteous living. It's an essential part of the preparation required to present your prayer request credibly to the Judge.

"Neither is there any creature that is not manifest in his sight, but all things are naked and opened unto the eyes of him with whom we have to do." (Hebrews 4:13).

There is nowhere to hide. God sees it all. Living right is important, don't you think? Here are a few verses to consider:

"Cast thy burden upon the Lord, and he shall sustain thee. He shall never suffer the righteous to be moved." (Psalm 55:22).

"I have been young, and now am old; yet have I not seen the righteous forsaken, nor his seed begging for bread." (Psalm 37:25).

I'm going to assume you care about your family. And if you have kids, then you care about their well-being. If so, then live righteously right now. Even beyond your prayers, God sees you and your lifestyle. Live your life before God as if it matters to those around you, because it does. How you live will affect others.

Consider the following verse.

"Thus saith the Lord, 'The heaven is my throne, and the earth is my footstool. Where is the house that ye build unto me? And where is the place of my rest? For all those things hath mine hand made, and all those things have been', saith the Lord: 'But to this man will

I look: even to him that is poor and of a contrite spirit, and trembleth at my word.'" (Isaiah 66:1-2).

And this one…

"The Lord is good, a stronghold in the day of trouble; and he knoweth them that trust in him." (Nahum 1:7)

Think about that verse. In your day of trouble (and those days will come), the LORD can be your stronghold. But only if you trust in Him. How do you display your trust in the LORD? Trust in Jesus first, then obey His commandments and live a righteous lifestyle. 'The effectual fervent prayer of a righteous man availeth much.'

THE PRAYER OF JABEZ

I would like to discuss two verses the Bible records about a man named Jabez and his prayer. I suppose you could focus on the words this man uttered. It's no doubt a solid prayer. But the conclusion I have drawn is that it's Jabez's lifestyle that propelled the prayer to a successful conclusion. It was the honorable lifestyle that God considered when Jabez entered God's courtroom with his request.

"And Jabez was more honorable than his brethren; and his mother called his name Jabez [that is, Sorrowful], saying, 'Because I bore him with sorrow.'
And Jabez called on the God of Israel, saying, 'Oh that Thou wouldest bless me indeed and enlarge my borders, and that Thine hand might be with me and that Thou wouldest keep me from evil, that it may not grieve me!' And God granted him that which he requested." (I Chronicles 4:9-10)

You could concoct the best sounding prayer ever devised, with all the right elements. But if you are living a wicked life and ignoring God's commands, then you are inhibiting your ability for your prayers to be heard. That's right, I said it. Unrighteous behavior will inhibit your prayers. The Bible is very clear on this point.

"He that turneth away his ear from hearing the law, even his prayer shall be abomination." (Proverbs 28:9)

This is a simple question: If God considers your prayer an abomination, then what are the odds of God granting your request?

"If I regard iniquity in my heart, the Lord will not hear me:" (Psalm 66:18)

In the book of Ezekiel, God poses a rhetorical question about the wicked and their prayers, then provides the remedy for mending their relationship status with God: repentance.

"And the word of the Lord came unto me, saying, 'Son of man, these men have set up their idols in their heart and put the stumbling block of their iniquity before their face. Should I be enquired of at all by them?'
Therefore say unto the house of Israel, 'Thus saith the Lord God; Repent, and turn yourselves from your idols; and turn away your faces from all your abominations.'" (Ezekiel 14:2-3,6).

In Isaiah, the LORD explains He can provide help, but the wicked lifestyle of those making their requests acts as a hinderance.

"Behold, the Lord's hand is not shortened, that it cannot save; neither His ear heavy, that it cannot hear. But your iniquities have separated between you and your God, and your sins have hid His face from you, that He will not hear." (Isaiah 59:1-2).

You see, the problem with obtaining answers to your prayers might not be God. The problem might be you and how you are living.

If you focus on uttering a multitude of words in prayer or spending extensive time in prayer, yet you don't devote time to cultivating a righteous lifestyle, then you are missing a crucial component of successful prayer. Fervent prayer and righteousness go hand in hand.

Before making a solemn prayer request for God's help, I find it important to engage in self-inspection. It's beneficial to compare your behavior to the Bible's instructions—and adjust your actions accordingly. However, the only way to attain this knowledge properly is to read the Bible for yourself. If you rarely read your Bible, even faithful church attendance will offer limited help. You must read the Bible—all of it—cover to cover.

JOB

Job was a righteous man. He was concerned for both his own righteousness and his family's. The Bible records:

"There was a man in the land of Uz, whose name was Job; and that man was perfect and upright, and one who feared God and eschewed evil.

And his sons went and feasted in their houses, every one his day, and sent and called for their three sisters to eat and to drink with them. And it was so, that when the days of their feasting were ended, Job sent and sanctified them, and rose up early in the morning and offered burnt offerings according to the number of them all; for Job said, 'It may be that my sons have sinned and cursed God in their hearts.' Thus did Job continually." (Job 1:1, 4-5).

I'd like to point out that Job repeatedly engaged in self-inspection for both him and his family to maintain righteous favor with God. We should learn from this example.

Following Job's pattern, I can prepare for the difficult times. I'm trying to emulate Job by striving for a lifestyle that is perfect and upright, by fearing God, and by eschewing (abstaining from and avoiding) evil. Then, when I have a prayer request for help, I can couple fervent prayer with my righteous lifestyle. I want to be ready to enter God's courtroom at a moment's notice, without the baggage of sin and iniquity being a hinderance.

A football coach once said, 'The only thing we can control is our level of intensity.' I suppose we can liken life to a football game. We are bound by universal rules, constantly facing opposition, and the referees don't always call things our way. As Christians, we can't control the instances of suffering and trouble that come our way. We can't control how God responds to our prayers. However, we can control whether we live rightly.

SALVATION & ETERNAL LIFE

Let's revisit the analogy of the courtroom. Imagine you have a court date at the local courthouse. However, in this specific case, your very life hangs in the balance. If the court acquits you, you may either walk free or, if convicted, they may sentence you to death. The stakes could not be higher.

Think for a moment. This holds immense significance. If this was genuinely transpiring in your life, then you would do everything in your power to build a robust defense, including hiring top notch lawyers. Opting to forgo professional legal representation would be a foolish decision. Society would mock you as a moron and an idiot. Your utter ignorance would be on full display.

Now, let's turn to reality. Everyone has a spiritual court date. The Bible proclaims:

"And as it is appointed unto men once to die, but after this the Judgment:" (Hebrews 9:27)

A.S.K.

Death is certain and unavoidable, and following that, a judgment also looms—equally certain and unavoidable. You will keep this appointment. You have no choice. Look into your own soul; you know this to be true. We will all stand before God the Judge one day soon.

Imagine entering the courtroom of God. Your very eternal life hangs in the balance. One of two fates awaits: a 'not guilty' verdict and the reward of eternal life, or a 'guilty' verdict and the punishment of an everlasting second death in hell.

If your plan is to represent yourself, then you are a fool. Any defense you attempt for yourself will fail. You require an advocate to plead your case before God, the Judge. The good news is that an advocate is available to assist you. A mediator stands between you and God. His name is Jesus Christ.

"For there is one God and one mediator between God and men, the man Christ Jesus" (I Timothy 2:5).

If you were facing a court date on earth, then finding a qualified defense attorney might be challenging. However, with Jesus Christ, He's the best and the only advocate available; the door is always open, and He doesn't charge a fee. As an added benefit, He has never lost a case.

There is already a prearranged agreement. If you accept Jesus as your advocate, he will represent you before God on your judgment day and guarantee a 'not guilty' verdict. Jesus bled and died on a Roman cross for your sins, but He conquered death and hell by resurrecting on the third day.

If you believe this truth, accept Jesus as your advocate, repent of your wickedness, and get baptized. You will die, but you will no longer have to fear judgment. This is the most important prayer you will ever utter. Humble yourself before God and accept His offer.

"And the Spirit and the bride say, 'Come'. And let him that heareth say, 'Come'. And let him that is athirst come; And whosoever will, let him take the Water of Life freely." (Revelation 22:17)

Otherwise, you can choose to represent yourself before God. This is foolish and will not end well. Don't be a fool.

2

According to God's Will

2

According to God's Will

Congratulations! You've made it to Chapter 2. Often, when people receive encouragement to lead a righteous life, they flee in the opposite direction. Unfortunately, it seems our American society has devolved into a phase reminiscent of the Old Testament, where 'every man does whatever is right in his own eyes.' Persuading someone to submit to God's commands is not something people will readily embrace.

But I hope you are different. If so, then read on!

The next few chapters were concepts I discovered through personal Bible study. Despite a lifetime of attending church, often two or three times a week, I did not learn these concepts from church sermons. Church sermons are brief and often lack the depth required to fully grasp what God has written.

LEGAL PRECEDENT

The first place to start is with a definition.

Legal Precedent: In common law legal systems, a precedent is a legal case that establishes a principle or rule. The court or other judicial bodies then use the rule when deciding later cases with similar issues or facts.

Let's return to the courtroom analogy. If you were preparing for a court date, you would present the facts and previous legal precedent in similar cases, along with your reasoning for why the judge should rule in your favor.

A.S.K.

There are volumes of books containing the legal precedents. If you have a skilled lawyer who can find a legal precedent matching your specific case, your odds of winning significantly increase.

Now, extend the concept of legal precedent to your prayer request. I find it helpful, and perhaps even necessary, to provide reasoning when making requests of God. I've observed that my prayers are more likely to be answered when I include reasoning in my request, rather than just asking for something. The most effective approach, in my experience, is to find a legal precedent within God's law book—the Bible.

If I can identify something in the Bible—a circumstance, a story, a prayer, or a direct statement—that shows how God responded, I consider these instances as a legal precedent of sorts. They serve as the foundation for why I believe God should answer my request.

If you study the prayers recorded in the Bible, you discover that nearly all of them (perhaps all of them) include an element of reasoning, explaining why God should respond. The Bible doesn't record anyone praying along the lines of, "I pray for Aunt Gertrude's festering gumboil, Amen."

Based on my experience, applying reasoning to prayer is quite effective. It serves the purpose of focusing your attention on the rationale behind your specific prayer. If you cannot convince yourself that your request has a valid reason for being answered, it should force you to reevaluate or change your prayer.

I will illustrate how this concept worked in the Bible and then share real-world examples of how it has worked in my life. When I understood this concept, a whole new world opened. I have a great deal of confidence in my requests when I can construct a reasonable case based on the Bible.

ACCORDING TO HIS WILL

Churchgoers frequently talk about the concept of God's will. Nevertheless, it seems that many people do not take the time to pause and contemplate God's will. To establish the foundation, let's start with a few verses.

"These things I have written unto you that believe in the name of the Son of God, that ye may know that ye have eternal life, and that ye may believe in the name of the Son of God. And this is the confidence that we have in Him: that if we ask anything according to His will, He heareth us. And if we know that He hears us, whatsoever we ask, we know that we have the petitions that we desired of Him." (I John 5:13-15)

This is a foundational statement: If we ask anything according to His will, God hears us and will grant our petitions.

"…but as the servants of Christ, doing the will of God from the heart, with good will doing service, as to the Lord and not to men," (Ephesians 6:6-7)

For too many years, I viewed God's will as a mystical and unknowable concept. It felt like the idea of 'whatever will be will be'. To put it another way, I was intertwining the concept of fate and God's will. Regardless of my circumstances, I mistakenly believed that God had predetermined the outcome. However, it's crucial to distinguish between the will of God and the concept of fate. The false god of fate is not our God.

So, how should we define the will of God? While I could delve into the theological depths, I believe the concept is rather straightforward. The Bible is God's will for our conduct and serves as a resource for contemplation, application in our lives, and support for our prayers.

I've often heard people submit a prayer request at church along these lines: "I would like to know God's will for my life." To clarify, it's my impression that asking to know 'God's will' is a mischaracterization. The genuine request is to seek God's guidance for a specific decision. Seeking God's help with challenging decisions is valid. Therefore, I'd like to distinguish between seeking help and the concept of God's will.

Consider a last will and testament—it's a documented set of instructions for the family to follow. I view the Bible in a similar light. It's God's written will, and God's children can apply these instructions to their lifestyle, choices, and prayers.

Let's look at some examples.

Is it appropriate for me to pray for immortal life here on earth? People request various forms of healing on prayer lists, so why not ask for the ultimate blessing of immortality? After all, why not aim for the highest goal, seeking not only improved health but also everlasting health?

Requesting immortality would be a waste of time. It's like the time a gentleman requested prayer for healing of a minor cut on his thumb. There's no need to pray for such a request because God has inherently designed the body to heal minor wounds. The same principle applies to a request for immortality. Our body will die—a universally acknowledged fact. And most importantly, God clearly articulated the fact in writing in Hebrews 9:27 "And as it is appointed unto men once to die…" If you pray for immortality, God will deny your request because it conflicts with His written will.

In the Bible, there are many declarations that can guide you in determining appropriate prayers. I began with the audacious notion of praying for immortality because the absurd can be the most effective way to make a point. It's so absurd that you probably never considered offering such a prayer.

Now, let's shift our focus to another area I suspect many have prayed about: wealth. If you're like me, you've asked God for riches.

So, let's discuss the subject of wealth for a minute. Should I pray to win the one-billion-dollar Powerball lottery? If I were to make such a request, I would need to determine rationally if there is a valid reason for God to answer my prayer. To begin the analysis of the appropriateness of praying for immense wealth, I should first consider what the Bible already says about such matters.

You see, I could form a prayer with lots of reasoning. For instance, I might pray, "It would be great if I could have $1B. You know I would help others. I would tithe, build a church, start an orphanage, help the poor—truly make a difference for the Kingdom of God, and so forth." All of this would be true, and I'd most likely do these things. However, the Bible offers some guidance to consider.

"Ye ask and receive not, because ye ask amiss, that ye may consume it upon your lusts." (James 4:3)

Uh-oh. You see, no matter how many noble intentions I would present to God, I cannot escape my underlying tendency to desire phenomenal riches so that I can consume it upon my own lusts. And besides that, if I were to give away most of the money to friends and family, or even to the church, there is the possibility that they would destroy themselves by consuming their newfound wealth in their own lusts.

Instead, we have God's will—written in the Bible.

"Two things have I required of Thee; deny me them not before I die: Remove far from me vanity and lies; give me neither poverty nor riches; feed me only food sufficient for me, lest I be full, and deny Thee, and say, 'Who is the Lord?' — or lest I be poor and steal, and take the name of my God in vain." (Proverbs 30:7-9)

Ask yourself this question: What would be the better life for you and your family - one with immense wealth or the one outlined in the Bible? I suggest you can find God's will within this narrow path—neither poverty nor riches, but by having just enough of what you need to be comfortably satisfied. The extremes of poverty and riches each bring their own problems. You don't want those problems.

PRAYERS WITH REASONING

Prayers recorded in the Bible include an element of reasoning. I don't think it would be practical to examine every prayer in the Bible as proof. This book would be too long. Now that I've directed your attention to the combination of reasoning and prayer, I hope that you'll start recognizing this pattern when you read the Bible on your own. To keep the book moving along, I offer two examples.

A.S.K.

JESUS' PRAYER ON THE CROSS

Jesus uttered a well-known prayer as he was dying on the cross as a sacrifice for our sins.

"Then Jesus said, 'Father, forgive them, for they know not what they do.'" (Luke 23:34)

In this prayer, Jesus asked God the Father to forgive, but also provided the reason for His request. God should forgive because they did not know what they were doing. I heard someone make this statement; after the religious leaders convicted the Son of God to death, they went off to say their prayers to God the Father. This serves as a poignant illustration of how both the religious leaders and the populace failed to comprehend the profound significance of the world-changing event in which they were partaking. They truly didn't know what they were doing.

THE HEALING OF HEZEKIAH

Hezekiah was a Jewish king during the waning years of the Kingdom of Judah. Unlike many of his predecessors, Hezekiah tried to serve God with a pure heart. I like this example because Hezekiah had a specific request for healing—an appeal that, in my observation, aligns with most requests found on a typical prayer list. The reason behind Hezekiah's request for healing is not only fascinating, but it also reinforces the importance of righteous living, a topic discussed in Chapter 1.

"In those days was Hezekiah sick unto death. And Isaiah the prophet, the son of Amoz, came unto him and said unto him, 'Thus saith the Lord: Set thine house in order, for thou shalt die and not live.' Then Hezekiah turned his face toward the wall, and prayed unto the Lord and said, 'Remember now, O Lord, I beseech Thee, how I have walked before Thee in truth and with a perfect heart, and have done that which is good in Thy sight.' And Hezekiah wept sorely. Then came the word of the Lord to Isaiah, saying, 'Go, and say to Hezekiah, Thus saith the Lord, the God of David thy father: I have heard thy prayer, I have seen thy tears. Behold, I will add unto thy days fifteen years.'" (Isaiah 38:1-5)

Hezekiah prayed, but it wasn't a simple recitation like, "I pray I don't die, Amen." Instead, Hezekiah offered a reason God should grant him more time, and that reason was his own righteous living. And it worked. Hezekiah encountered a storm of life, his impending death, and he was prepared to pray because of his righteous conduct, which he then used as the reason for his request.

The effectual fervent prayer of a righteous man is powerful. Hezekiah's fervency was evident in his profound brokenness. He didn't cry; he wept sorely. It was deep mourning. Notice that God responds by saying two things. I heard your prayer. I saw your tears. God recognized two facets of Hezekiah's character—his righteousness and the sincerity of his plea. God's response is consistent with the character of God, because He has compassion for each of us. He is merciful, kind, and patient. Hezekiah's prayer request, which was rooted in righteousness and sincerity, received a positive response from God.

This example holds wide-ranging implications because, as we age, the likelihood of encountering health problems increase. Since we know this to be true, we should prepare ourselves for future health challenges in the present. When the time comes, will you be able to offer a prayer like Hezekiah's, and it will be true about yourself? Will you value extra time on the earth to the point of weeping sore before God? If so, then there's a chance God might grant your request as well, just as He has done in the past. It's written in His will as an example. While it's not a guarantee, because God may have better plans for you, it can serve as a framework for approaching God when the doctor comes along with bad news.

What happens if God declines your request for healing? I believe the Bible provides an alternative request: pray for peace. In the words of the Bible, it would be a prayer for a peace that passes all understanding—a peace that will confound anyone in your sphere of influence.

"And the peace of God, which passeth all understanding, shall keep your hearts and minds through Christ Jesus." (Philippians 4:7)

A.S.K.

The peace of God is God's will for you. If you face certain death, then request personal peace. The rationale is straightforward, and I'd use this verse as the basis to develop a prayer request along these lines: "God, faced with death, grant me the peace that passes all understanding, so that my faith in you serves as a testament to my family, the medical professionals, and those around me. You stated in the Bible that my faith can be the evidence of things that are unseen, and the substance of things hoped for. Please use my death to draw people closer to you and convert a sinner from their wicked ways. Amen."

IT'S OUR TURN

I read the Bible a lot. I find it to be an invaluable source of wisdom. However, it truly came to life when I began experimenting with the concepts and guidance I discovered, and then applying these to my everyday life.

Roughly 18 years ago, my father's diagnosis of prostate cancer prompted one of my early experiments. Initially, the news was upsetting, and I turned to God in prayer.

Yet, as I continued to pray, something troubled me about my prayer request. Stepping back to examine my discomfort, I realized I didn't have a precise understanding of what I was praying for. I asked myself: "What is my specific prayer request? As I approach God, what exactly am I seeking?"

I wondered, "Was I praying for his healing?" If so, it would take years to know the outcome. In the meantime, I'd be battling worry and fear about the future continuously.

This introspection led me to ask myself, "Is worrying and fretting about my father's cancer an appropriate behavior for a Christian? Is worry and anxiety the path of my life now?"

At the root of my prayer, there was an undercurrent of fear—fear of the unknown, fear of the future, fear of my father's illness, and the possibility of his passing. The Bible is critical of the fearful. Jesus once asked his disciples, "Why are you fearful?" and then linked their fear to a lack of faith (Matthew 8:26 and Mark 4:40). Revelation 21:8 describes those who will have their part in the lake which burns with fire and brimstone, starting the list with 'the fearful'. The list also contains the unbelieving, the abominable, the murders and warmongers, the sorcerers and idolaters, and all liars. Yet the list starts with 'the fearful.'

These nuances in the Bible never cease to fascinate me. Fearfulness would not top my list of human evils, but the Bible illuminates a truth here that I would never grasp on my own. The Bible teaches me I should not be full of worry or fear—except for fearing God—because it is a fearful thing to fall into the hands of the living God who can destroy both soul and body in hell (Hebrews 10:27, Matthew 10:28). Beyond this, God does not desire me to be fearful; God's ways are peace and joy, not worry and fear.

Given that fear is wrong, I began contemplating how to apply this knowledge to my situation. Naturally, the circumstances were generating worry and fear, so I started considering what circumstances could help ease my concerns.

Keep in mind that while I'm pondering these ideas, I'm consistently reading my Bible daily. As I read, thoughts take shape, forming a kind of mental wall. Knowledge accumulates, brick by brick, until there is a full wall of understanding to contemplate. Through personal experience, I know God speaks through the Bible if you'll take the time to read it daily. Gaining the true value from the Bible demands dedication to daily reading. It sometimes feels as though my interaction with God increased once I showed commitment to His word. This isn't a scriptural statement, but an observation from my life. Have I told you to read your Bible enough already? A friend once told me he knows the perfect words to be written on my tombstone: "READ YOUR BIBLE." If you were to sum up my life into three words, those are the right three words.

I noticed that reading the Bible regularly has a transformative effect on the mind. You'll think in different ways and think different thoughts. Novel ideas and concepts will form that never occurred to you before. You will become acquainted with wisdom. Over recent years, as I've watched events unfold, I think the Bible has, in a sense, immunized me against the lies prevalent in our society. Many of my fellow citizens fall prey to all kinds of lies and propaganda, and I find myself bewildered by their skewed reasoning. Jesus promised to give His followers the Holy Spirit, using the descriptive words, "However when He, the SPIRIT OF TRUTH, is come, He will guide you into all TRUTH" (John 16:13). In my experience, the Spirit of Truth hangs around the Bible quite a bit while I'm reading.

A.S.K.

While I contemplated my prayer request in relation to the context of overcoming the fear of my father's cancer, a few verses from my reading stood out.

"Come unto Me all ye that labor and are heavy laden, and I will give you rest. Take My yoke upon you and learn of Me, for I am meek and lowly in heart, and ye shall find rest unto your souls. For My yoke is easy, and My burden is light." (Matthew 11:28-30)

"Likewise the Spirit also helpeth our infirmities; for we know not what we should pray for as we ought, but the Spirit itself maketh intercession for us with groanings which cannot be uttered. And He that searcheth the hearts knoweth what is the mind of the Spirit, because He maketh intercession for the saints according to the will of God. And we know that all things work together for good to those who love God, to those who are the called according to His purpose." (Romans 8:26-28)

These verses teach me it's God's will that I find rest for my soul. If this is true (and it is), then I should be able to find rest, even in the face of something as daunting as the potential death of my father from cancer.

These verses also state that God would assist us in praying during times like these. There are moments when reason fails, and all you can do is ask God to help you pray. Finally, God promises that if we love Him, He will work out all things for good. Love is a complex concept that is hard to define and even harder to measure, but I am certain that I love God's Word. The Bible is more precious to me than anything in life, and I don't make that statement lightly. In a way, loving God's Word intertwines with loving God, as He describes Himself as, "In the beginning was the Word, and the Word was with God, and the Word was God." (John 1:1).

Given these considerations, my logic formed along this path. First, to understand HOW to pray, I needed to know WHAT to pray. Second, to know WHAT to pray, I needed to know the eventual OUTCOME. If I knew the outcome would be the death of my father, then my prayers and pleas would be for a miraculous healing. If the outcome would be a successful cancer treatment and eventual clean bill of health, then there would be no need for additional prayers, and I'd be free from worry, anxiety and fear.

My initial prayer request underwent a transformation; it was now a request for knowledge. Isn't that an interesting change of approach? You might think I'm smart, but it's wisdom I drew directly from the Bible and applied to my situation.

After thinking about how to phrase my request, I offered a prayer that was like this: "Lord, as You are aware, my father has cancer. Naturally, I'm worried and lack the ability within myself to overcome this nagging fear. You wrote that if I was heavy laden, that You could give me rest. I'm coming to You hoping You can provide a lighter burden. Maybe I'm not praying the way I should, so help me know how to pray. I believe that You can work all things out for good if I love You. These things lead me to the conclusion that if I know the outcome of my father's cancer, if I could know now that it's nothing to worry about and that he'll respond to treatment just fine and live many more years, then the worry and fear would be gone. Please let me know the outcome Jesus. Amen."

As we'll explore in the upcoming chapters, I added fasting (from food) to my prayer. I really wanted an answer, and I proved it by not eating. Similar to the combination of Hezekiah's prayer and his tears, I wanted God to hear my request and witness my fasting.

Part of the reason I'm writing this book is that I had been experimenting with this concept for a while. However, this request was major league, the ultimate confirmation I needed to have confidence in the effectiveness of this method for crafting serious prayers.

God's reply didn't take long. It was just a handful of days, and I remember the exact spot I was standing when I received a word from the Lord. I was on the landing of the split-level staircase leading to my home office. At that moment, I knew with certainty—my father would recover, and the prostate cancer would not claim his life.

How did the answer come? The process may be difficult for a non-Christian to comprehend, but if you are a Christian, you may find this experience familiar.

God communicates in various ways, primarily through reading the Bible. In this specific case, the closest analogy I can offer is that of a computer. Picture my brain as a computer, not connected to any external network, running its internal dialogue of thoughts. Now, consider what happens when you insert a

A.S.K.

USB drive into a personal computer. The Windows operating system recognizes this new USB device as an outside entity. In this analogy, my brain is a self-contained system processing its own internal 'walking up my staircase' thoughts, when suddenly, something akin to inserting a USB drive occurs. It's not a voice, as in an audible statement from God; rather, it's like the rapid insertion of new information or knowledge from an external source. In a fraction of a second, this new knowledge entered my mind, and it was the assurance that my father would be fine.

With this knowledge came a sense of certainty and peace. I would have wagered my next paycheck on it. I knew deep in my soul that it was true.

You see, this experience is hard to explain. It's somewhat like describing the Grand Canyon. You can look at pictures and hear stories from others who have visited, but you won't fully grasp its majesty until you see it in person. For those of you who have similar encounters with God's responses to your prayers, you understand what I mean. If you can't relate, I encourage you to put the concepts outlined in this book into practice. I'm confident that as you do, you'll understand.

After the initial certainty and celebration of having my prayer request answered, the next hurdle arrived: doubt. Of course it was. I'm human.

Doubt presented a very different dilemma. I began questioning myself. Had I genuinely heard from God, or was it merely wishful thinking? Should I stop praying for my father's cancer altogether? After all, if he was going to be fine, continuing to pray would expose my doubt.

Ultimately, I chose to believe. I figured that any other course of action would be a betrayal. So, I stopped praying about it. I didn't add the request to the prayer list at church. I even forgot about my father's cancer altogether. I had received the light yoke Jesus promised and found rest for my soul. I had cast my burden upon Him and emerged burden-free. The fear and worry were gone.

As time passed, the hospital scheduled my father for prostate surgery. On the day of the operation, his pastor arrived to pray over him. As the pastor prayed, I thought to myself, "I should stop him now; I already know the outcome." However, I didn't share my knowledge or my prayer process with anyone else. I was still learning to trust God, much like the young Samuel serving under the High Priest Eli.

The surgery was lengthy, and as I waited with my mother, she grew increasingly agitated and concerned. To calm her, I reassured her that there was no reason to worry. Eventually, she blurted out, "How do you know there is nothing to worry about? Anything could go wrong!"

And there it was. How did I know that all would be well? I knew, but I couldn't explain. Even if I had described the entire process of seeking God that led to an answer, I doubted it would have provided her any comfort. Like Ecclesiastes teaches, there is a time for everything, and that wasn't the time to explain.

As you probably deduced, time has provided the evidence. My father survived prostate cancer, and it has not reoccurred in all these years.

This entire story became possible because I began using the Bible as my legal precedent to help form my prayers. If I could find examples in the Bible relevant to my situation, I could form a prayer request that aligned with God's will. Prayer and the Bible go hand in hand.

THIS ONE IS FREE

I'll provide you with another example that can apply to your life. Let's assume you are single and would like to find a soulmate. The first step is to lead a righteous life (it matters). Then, you can form a prayer like the following (note to parents—you can easily adapt this to pray for future spouses for your children).

"Lord, I'd prefer not to be single much longer. But in our culture, finding a solid Christian soulmate is difficult. You instruct us in II Corinthians 6:14 not to be unequally yoked together with unbelievers, and this is especially true of marriage. You ask the rhetorical question, 'What fellowship has righteousness with unrighteousness, and what communion has light with darkness?'. I agree with Your observation. Therefore, finding a solid Christian to marry is necessary. However, finding a good, wholesome spouse is increasingly difficult. The eligible candidates within my sphere are rather limited. You also state in the Ecclesiastes 4:9-11 that two are better than one because if one falls, the other can help lift them up. I'd like that kind of help and support in my life. I desire to have someone to love and who loves me in return. Someone to stand with me through the good times and the bad. You also instructed us in Genesis

9:7 to be fruitful and multiply, which means…You know what it means. You also said early in Genesis 2:18 that it is not good that the man should be alone. I believe these things. So, I ask You to bring along someone that would make a good spouse that can help build a strong God-fearing family. Without Your help, my searching is vanity, and I risk falling into the trap that Solomon found himself in, where his wives turned away his heart from You. I'm looking for You to provide. Sincerely, your humble servant. Amen."

Notice the number of Bible references I crammed into that brief prayer? It's a prayer that aligns with God's will. The Bible tells us that if we pray according to His will, He hears us and grants our petitions. Do you believe in this promise? If so, then pray!

I want to emphasize that everything I am sharing intertwines with faith. If you put prayer into practice, you'll witness things unfolding. You'll experience a growing confidence, just as I did, which directly translates into an increased faith. Once you reach out to God, and He reaches back, you'll see tangible changes taking place in your life.

For many years, churches encouraged me to be a witness for Christ, but it was a struggle. However, everything changed when I figured out prayer. Prayer works. There is indeed a God on the other end who engages with me. My faith grew, and I'm willing to tell anyone that God is real, that He loves us, and that you would be wise to pay attention to His Word before it's too late.

Hopefully, this book proves to be beneficial. As the saying goes, "Teach a man to fish and he'll eat for a lifetime," right? Teach a righteous person to pray fervently, and they'll become highly effective. I like to think that this can indeed change the world.

BONUS SECTION!

Everyone likes a bonus, right? Besides the two Biblical examples mentioned earlier in this chapter, I've selected three for further exploration. So, if you've found Chapter 2 enjoyable, then read on. Otherwise, skip to Chapter 3 for more of the story.

BONUS EXAMPLE THREE

Hezekiah, King of Judah, had yet another urgent prayer request. The Assyrians were advancing to lay waste to Jerusalem. A letter from the Assyrians arrived, detailing the impending doom of Judah. But Hezekiah didn't need a letter; he had already heard of the surrounding nations falling like dominos before the Assyrians. They were unbeatable.

Once again, King Hezekiah combined prayer with a physical action. He took the Assyrian letter and spread it out before God, then offered his prayer.

"And Hezekiah received the letter from the hand of the messengers and read it; and Hezekiah went up unto the house of the Lord and spread it before the Lord. And Hezekiah prayed unto the Lord, saying, 'O Lord of hosts, God of Israel, who dwellest between the cherubims, Thou art the God, even Thou alone, of all the kingdoms of the earth; Thou hast made heaven and earth. Incline Thine ear, O Lord, and hear; open Thine eyes, O Lord, and see; and hear all the words of Sennacherib, who hath sent to reproach the living God. In truth, Lord, the kings of Assyria have laid waste all the nations and their countries, and have cast their gods into the fire; for they were no gods, but the work of men's hands, wood and stone. Therefore they have destroyed them. Now therefore, O Lord our God, save us from his hand, that all the kingdoms of the earth may know that Thou art the Lord, even Thou only.'" (Isaiah 37:14-20)

At the end of the prayer lies the reason for God to grant the request, and it's an interesting one. King Hezekiah thought it was a unique opportunity for God to remind the kingdoms of earth that He is the one and only God. The Lord granted his request.

I thought about explaining the rest of Hezekiah's story, but as I've mentioned, it's essential that you read the Bible. I encourage you to find the story and read of the power of God on full display.

A.S.K.

BONUS EXAMPLE FOUR

Here is a remarkable tale: there was an Israelite widow. Her husband was a prophet during his lifetime, but after his passing, the widow was drowning in massive debt. The debt was so overwhelming that the creditors threatened to take away her young sons to be bondmen, forced to work off her debt.

In her desperation, the widow cries out to Elisha for help.

"Now there cried a certain woman of the wives of the sons of the prophets unto Elisha, saying, 'Thy servant my husband is dead, and thou knowest that thy servant feared the Lord; and the creditor hath come to take unto him my two sons to be bondmen.'" (II Kings 4:1)

Again, this example draws upon the concept of righteous living for its reasoning, but with a unique twist. Here, the widow relied on the righteous living of her deceased husband. And it worked! Elisha instructed the widow and her sons to borrow as many empty vessels as possible, close the door of their house, take their single cruse of oil, and start filling the borrowed vessels. They obey the command, and the oil multiplied. The single cruse of oil fills every borrowed vessel and did not run dry until it fills them all to the brim. Elisha then instructed her to sell the oil, pay off her debts, and survive with the rest.

BONUS EXAMPLE FIVE

Judah faced imminent destruction from an invading army composed of three different nations. The army was so large that it would easily overwhelm Judah. There was no hope. In a matter of days, the invading army would destroy their cities, slaughter their men and women, and carry off their virgins as spoils of war.

The final and only option was to call upon the Lord.

"It came to pass after this also, that the children of Moab and the children of Ammon, and with them others besides the Ammonites, came against Jehoshaphat to battle. Then there came some who told Jehoshaphat, saying, 'There cometh a great multitude against thee from beyond the sea on this side of Syria; and behold, they are in Hazazontamar, which is Engedi.'

And Jehoshaphat feared, and set himself to seek the Lord, and proclaimed a fast throughout all Judah. And Judah gathered themselves together to ask help of the Lord; even out of all the cities of Judah they came to seek the Lord.

And Jehoshaphat stood in the congregation of Judah and Jerusalem, in the house of the Lord, before the new court, and said, 'O Lord God of our fathers, art not Thou God in heaven? And rulest not Thou over all the kingdoms of the heathen? And in Thine hand is there not power and might, so that none is able to withstand Thee? Art not Thou our God, who didst drive out the inhabitants of this land before Thy people Israel, and gavest it to the seed of Abraham Thy friend for ever? And they dwelt therein, and have built Thee a sanctuary therein for Thy name, saying, 'If, when evil cometh upon us, as the sword, judgment, or pestilence, or famine, we stand before this house and in Thy presence (for Thy name is in this house), and cry unto Thee in our affliction, then Thou wilt hear and help.' And now, behold, the children of Ammon and Moab and Mount Seir, whom Thou wouldest not let Israel invade when they came out of the land of Egypt, but they turned from them and destroyed them not; Behold, I say, how they reward us by coming to cast us out of Thy possession, which Thou hast given us to inherit. O our God, wilt Thou not judge them? For we have no might against this great company that cometh against us, neither know we what to do; but our eyes are upon Thee.'

And all Judah stood before the Lord with their little ones, their wives, and their children." (II Chronicles 20:1-13)

A.S.K.

All the essential elements of a successful prayer are present. There was a reasoned plea, grounded in the promise of God written in King Solomon's prayer from the temple's dedication. Jehoshaphat recalled their nation's obedience to God's command to spare Ammon and Moab during their exodus from Egypt, as well as God's promise to give the land as their inheritance (which was now in jeopardy). They presented themselves visually before the Lord. Notice the wording of the last verse: 'All Judah stood before the Lord, with their little ones, their wives, and their children.' God saw them.

And their approach worked. God granted their request. You can explore the full story on your own, but in short, the three invading armies descended into a civil war, ultimately annihilating themselves. Instead of being destroyed, Judah inherited all the spoils of these defeated armies, amassing an abundance of wealth that took days to collect. In a matter of days, the nation's outlook transformed from impending doom to overwhelming prosperity.

A.S.K.

3

Seek - Knock

A.S.K.

3

Seek - Knock

Until now, I've focused on the 'ask' aspect of prayer, but there are many other facets related to 'seeking' and 'knocking' that warrant exploration. Uttering words is one thing; however, adding action and sacrifice into our request is another.

According to the Bible, one form of action in prayer involves fasting from food, and in specific cases, clothing oneself in sackcloth and ashes. In my experience, these are vital components to prayer when confronting a formidable challenge.

Have you ever prayed and felt as if nothing was happening? You've conducted self-inspection and made confessions, but a sense of impediment or hinderance persists. If that is the case, my advice is to push the boundaries and add fasting to your request. If you're familiar with the Bible, you'll notice that serious prayers often include an element of fasting.

The great prophet Elijah said:

"But he himself went a day's journey into the wilderness, and came and sat down under a juniper tree; and he requested for himself that he might die, and said, 'It is enough! Now, O Lord, take away my life, for I am not better than my fathers.'" (I Kings 19:4)

I often ponder the statement, 'I am not better than my fathers.' If the ancient people of the Bible would periodically fast, and in times of great mourning or fear, clothe themselves in sackcloth and ashes, then why not me? I'm no better than my fathers. The Bible is clear these practices had an impact back then, so why not now? Why not me? Is it because I'm too modern, with my indoor running water, hot showers, and fully stocked grocery stores, that fasting and sackcloth are beneath me?

Just because church teachings haven't emphasized these points doesn't render them obsolete. The Bible is directly teaching me these principles. Just because I've never heard a single person talk about wearing sackcloth as part of a difficult prayer doesn't discredit the idea. Perhaps we've all simply forgotten. Maybe something has blinded us, and we need a reminder.

As with all things, I am a skeptic. I rarely accept anything solely based on proclamation. Men are liars and full of corruption, so I've always believed that it's wise to be skeptical. Therefore, when the idea of fasting and sackcloth crossed my mind, I realized that the only way to determine their validity was to put them into practice myself—to experiment.

FASTING

I'm sure you've come across the phrase WWJD (What Would Jesus Do). Well, Jesus would pray privately and fast.

"And when He had fasted forty days and forty nights, He afterward hungered." (Matthew 4:2)

Biblical fasting is abstaining from food. While you must drink water, as you can't go many days without it before dying, I've witnessed the mistake of people attempting to substitute food fasting with abstaining from something else, an idea I reject. Fasting from food is a unique spiritual experience.

In one sense, it's your spiritual side temporarily taking control over your physical side, and your physical side will rebel because the body doesn't enjoy being hungry. Try going without food for a few days, and you'll gain a heightened realization of the abundance of food advertisements.

A.S.K.

Amidst the constant temptation of food, your hunger serves another purpose—it acts as a reminder to pray. We all get busy with life. The demands of work and family are ever-present. A prayer request can often get lost in the noise. However, if you have a serious prayer request, those hunger pangs cut through the noise and refocus your attention on prayer. They might even keep you awake at night, lying in bed, hungry and in deep prayer.

Now, if I were to decide to fast from roller coaster riding for an extended period (because, you know, I'm spiritual like that), it wouldn't translate well into prayer. In fact, I haven't been on one for eight years, and it has not affected my spiritual well-being. No matter what you attempt to substitute for fasting from food, it will never replicate the same effect. I can give up plenty of things, like lettuce and exercise, but they never generate the same sense of urgency.

I understand that fasting from food might not be workable for everyone because of health reasons or other factors. God knows you, so that won't surprise Him or limit His power. However, this is where I think sackcloth and ashes can step in to fill the gap. What is sackcloth, you ask? It's essentially burlap, readily available in most fabric stores. In my case, I purchased some, cut a hole for my head, and wore it like a robe. I did this in the privacy of my home. After all, Jesus commanded us to pray privately.

"Moreover when ye fast, be not, as the hypocrites, of a sad countenance. For they disfigure their faces, that they may appear unto men to fast. Verily I say unto you, they have their reward. But thou, when thou fastest, anoint thine head and wash thy face, that thou appear not unto men to fast, but unto thy Father who is in secret; and thy Father, who seeth in secret, shall reward thee openly." (Matthew 6:16-18)

I didn't wear a shirt under the burlap. Just as hunger pains serve as a reminder to pray, the rough texture of burlap against your skin serves as a constant reminder to pray. Burlap is exceptionally coarse and uncomfortable (not recommended for fashion wear).

Then there are the ashes. The Bible occasionally mentions a combination of sackcloth and ashes. Creating ashes is a straightforward process—just a few burnt pages from a newspaper will suffice.

What I discovered through this process, particularly the act of creating ashes and then rubbing them on my head, was profound humility. I cannot emphasize this enough—it is deeply humbling. I hope that you'll consider experimenting with these practices on your own. If you do, you will see for yourself.

But perhaps that is the point, the essence of it all. One cannot overstate the significance of humility before God. Note the term 'in the sight' in the passage below.

"Humble yourselves in the sight of the Lord, and He shall lift you up." (James 4:10)

"Likewise, ye younger, submit yourselves unto the elder. Yea, all of you be subject one to another, and be clothed with humility; for 'God resisteth the proud, and giveth grace to the humble.'" (I Peter 5:5)

"For whosoever exalteth himself shall be abased, and he that humbleth himself shall be exalted." (Luke 14:11)

As you experiment with these concepts on your own, you'll learn to recognize the need for fasting. What has worked for me is when a prayer lingers without a response, or I sense a hinderance of some sort, as if my prayer is merely rebounding off the ceiling. When this happens, I'll often start fasting. With the combination of prayer and fasting, I've never failed to receive an answer of some sort.

Jesus encountered a situation where prayer alone was not sufficient.

"And when they had come to the multitude, there came to Him a man, kneeling down to Him and saying, 'Lord, have mercy on my son, for he is lunatic and sorely vexed; for ofttimes he falleth into the fire and oft into the water. And I brought him to Thy disciples, and they could not cure him.'

Then Jesus answered and said, 'O faithless and perverse generation, how long shall I be with you? How long shall I suffer you? Bring him hither to Me.' And Jesus rebuked the devil, and he departed out of him, and the child was cured from that very hour.

Then came the disciples to Jesus apart and said, 'Why could we not cast him out?' And Jesus said unto them, 'Because of your unbelief; for verily I say unto you, if ye have faith as a grain of mustard seed, ye shall say unto this mountain, 'Remove hence to yonder place,' and it shall remove. And nothing shall be impossible unto you. However this kind goeth not out but by prayer and fasting.'" (Matthew 17:14-21)

Some Bible versions omit the phrase 'and fasting' from the last verse. Don't be fooled. Fasting is precisely the focal point of the story. Sometimes prayer alone isn't sufficient, and fasting is required.

I'd also like to mention that sackcloth is not a gimmick. I suppose attitude is everything. If you think wearing sackcloth is some sort of shortcut, then you've missed the point entirely. According to my observations of the patterns in the Bible, people would save sackcloth for desperate times when their souls were vexed. Only when you hit rock bottom, with no hope or alternatives, will your attitude align with the humility that sackcloth outwardly symbolizes. You can't pretend to be broken by wearing sackcloth. You are broken and therefore wear sackcloth to match the condition of your heart.

"My soul is also sore vexed, but Thou, O Lord, how long? Return, O Lord, deliver my soul! O save me for Thy mercies' sake! I am weary with my groaning; all the night I make my bed to swim, I water my couch with my tears. Mine eye is consumed because of grief; it waxeth old because of all mine enemies. The Lord hath heard my supplication; the Lord will receive my prayer." (Psalm 6:3-4, 6-7, 9)

Next, let's explore some practical examples from the Bible that illustrate the combination of prayer, fasting, sackcloth, and ashes.

FORGIVENESS – KING AHAB

The first example is King Ahab, possibly one of the most wicked individuals to have ever lived. He was wicked to the core. Here is how the Bible describes him:

"But there was none like unto Ahab, who sold himself to work wickedness in the sight of the Lord, whom Jezebel his wife stirred up. And he did very abominably in following idols, according to all things as did the Amorites, whom the Lord cast out before the children of Israel." (I Kings 21:25-26)

The LORD's patience had run out for King Ahab, and God sent a message of doom to this wicked man.

"And Ahab said to Elijah, 'Hast thou found me, O mine enemy?' And he answered, 'I have found thee, because thou hast sold thyself to work evil in the sight of the Lord. 'Behold, I will bring evil upon thee, and will take away thy posterity, and will cut off from Ahab him that urinates against the wall, and him that is shut up and left in Israel. And will make thine house like the house of Jeroboam the son of Nebat, and like the house of Baasha the son of Ahijah, for the provocation wherewith thou hast provoked Me to anger and made Israel sin." And of Jezebel also spoke the Lord, saying, 'The dogs shall eat Jezebel by the wall of Jezreel. Him of Ahab that dieth in the city the dogs shall eat, and him that dieth in the field shall the fowls of the air eat.'" (I Kings 21:20-24)

Doom on you and your family. It's quite a curse. What's interesting to note is that King Ahab had a couple of choices here. He could have easily scoffed at the prediction and ignored the warning, as some other Kings of Israel had done, one of which burned a written prophetic warning in the fireplace (Jeremiah 36:22-24).

The pivotal point here is belief. King Ahab believed. He believed the words of the prophet Elijah. He believed there was a God in heaven with the power to execute judgment and justice. And because he believed, he responded with fasting and sackcloth.

"And it came to pass, when Ahab heard those words, that he rent his clothes and put sackcloth upon his flesh, and fasted and lay in sackcloth, and went about dispiritedly.
And the word of the Lord came to Elijah the Tishbite, saying, 'Seest thou how Ahab humbleth himself before Me? Because he humbleth himself before Me, I will not bring the evil in his days; but in his son's days will I bring the evil upon his house.'" (I Kings 21:27-29)

King Ahab, despite his many failings, sought God's forgiveness through fasting and sackcloth. In keeping with His character, God honored Ahab's act of contrition and humbleness, leading to a change in His judgment of doom upon Ahab. God forgave this wicked man.

If we pivot to our own time, we also have warnings of personal doom from the prophets written in the Bible. The Bible's message is simple. Jesus said:

"...that whosoever believeth in Him should not perish, but have eternal life.
He that believeth in Him is not condemned; but He that believeth not is condemned already, because he hath not believed in the name of the only begotten Son of God.
And this is the condemnation: that Light is come into the world, and men loved darkness rather than light, because their deeds were

evil. For every one that doeth evil hateth the light, neither cometh to the light, lest his deeds should be reproved." (John 3:15, 18-20)

"And death and hell were cast into the lake of fire. This is the second death. And whosoever was not found written in the Book of Life was cast into the lake of fire." (Revelation 20:14-15)

This is a written warning of doom, and there are many others. Jesus talked more about hell than he did heaven. It's a warning. Every one of us, just like King Ahab, faces a choice. Do we believe the words of Jesus and the prophets? Do we believe there is a God in heaven with the power to execute judgment and justice? If so, will we beg His forgiveness? Or will we scoff at His word and mock His followers?

"Enter ye in at the strait gate, for wide is the gate and broad is the way that leadeth to destruction, and many there be who go in thereat. Because strait is the gate, and narrow is the way which leadeth unto life, and few there be that find it." (Matthew 7:12-13)

FORGIVENESS - NINEVAH

Nineveh was a city steeped in wickedness. Like the situation with King Ahab, God's patience had run out. So, God sent the prophet Jonah to the city with a message of doom.

"And Jonah began to enter into the city a day's journey, and he cried and said, 'Yet forty days, and Nineveh shall be overthrown.'
So the people of Nineveh believed God, and proclaimed a fast and put on sackcloth, from the greatest of them even to the least of them. For word came unto the king of Nineveh; and he arose from his throne, and he laid his robe from him, and covered himself with sackcloth and sat in ashes. And he caused it to be proclaimed and published through Nineveh by the decree of the

king and his nobles, saying, 'Let neither man nor beast, herd nor flock, taste anything; let them not feed, nor drink water. But let man and beast be covered with sackcloth and cry mightily unto God. Yea, let them turn everyone from his evil way, and from the violence that is in their hands. Who can tell if God will turn and repent, and turn away from His fierce anger, that we perish not?'

And God saw their works, that they turned from their evil way. And God repented of the evil that He had said that He would do unto them, and He did it not." (Jonah 3:4-10)

All the elements of prayer are present here. It began with the people believing in God's word, and then progressed to repentance from their wicked ways, a firm commitment to change, fasting, sackcloth, and ashes. In response, God heard their prayers, saw their acts of contrition, and granted a reprieve.

DELIVERANCE & PROTECTION FROM HARD TIMES - EZRA

There are hard times in life. Ezra lived during such times in the generation following the destruction of Jerusalem. Yet God had a plan, and He entrusted Ezra with rebuilding the city. However, enemies and lethal resistance loomed. Naturally, Ezra was worried, but he had a secret weapon.

"Then I proclaimed a fast there at the river of Ahava, that we might humble ourselves before our God, to seek of Him a right way for us and for our little ones, and for all our substance. For I was ashamed to request of the king a band of soldiers and horsemen to help us against the enemy on the way, because we had spoken unto the king, saying, 'The hand of our God is upon all those for good who seek Him, but His power and His wrath is against all those who forsake Him.'

So we fasted and besought our God for this; and He was entreated by us. Then we departed from the river of Ahava on the twelfth day of the first month to go unto Jerusalem; and the hand of our God was upon us, and He delivered us from the hand of the enemy and from such as lay in wait by the way. And we came to Jerusalem, and stayed there three days." (Ezra 8:21-23, 31-32)

Ezra believed it would be inappropriate to rely on the king's soldiers for protection. Instead, he thought it would be a stronger demonstration of faith if he showed his belief in God through action. Once again, notice that Ezra incorporated Bible verses into his prayer (as we've discussed in previous chapters), but he also included fasting.

DELIVERANCE & PROTECTION FROM HARD TIMES - ESTHER

The book of Esther recounts a time when the King of Persia issued a decree to all 127 providences. This decree established a day when the citizens of the kingdom could kill all the Jews and seize ownership of their property. Imagine a government granting legal approval to kill a small percentage of the population and confiscate their wealth. Such a decree would create a significant greed incentive for the general population to take part, especially against such a small minority with minimal protection. Faced with this impending genocide, here is how the Jewish people in the Persian empire responded.

"When Mordecai perceived all that was done, Mordecai rent his clothes and put on sackcloth with ashes, and went out into the midst of the city and cried with a loud and a bitter cry, and came even before the king's gate; for none might enter into the king's gate clothed with sackcloth. And in every province whithersoever the king's commandment and his decree came, there was great mourning among the Jews, and fasting and weeping and wailing; and many lay in sackcloth and ashes." (Esther 4:1-3)

Amid the mourning, Mordecai had an idea. As Providence would have it, Mordecai had raised his niece Esther, who had become the Queen. However, Mordecai and Esther had concealed their family relationship, and no one knew

Esther was Jewish. Mordecai approached Queen Esther with a request to speak to the king about his decree. But a significant hurdle loomed. No one could approach the king unless he extended a specific invitation; there were no unscheduled appointments. If you attempted to see the king without an appointment, he might grant you an audience, but he also had the power to execute you on the spot. The king's time was precious. Naturally, Esther was afraid to approach the king, but she agreed to do so under one condition.

"Then Esther bade them return Mordecai this answer: 'Go, gather together all the Jews who are present in Shushan, and fast ye for me; and neither eat nor drink three days, night or day. I also and my maidens will fast likewise. And so will I go in unto the king, which is not according to the law; and if I perish, I perish.'" (Esther 4:15-16)

The commitment to prayer and fasting worked. Esther played a pivotal role in initiating the deliverance of all the Jews throughout the vast Persian empire. God saw and heard the Jew's prayers and fasting.

There are moments in life that are bigger than routine prayers. Ideally, one would hope to avoid such dire circumstances altogether. However, if you find yourself in such a situation, the examples in the Bible offer valuable guidance.

SICKNESS

Health is an immensely significant part of life. In the book of Job, Satan proclaims, 'Skin for skin, yea, all that a man hath will he give for his life.' Disease and sickness can affect both you and your loved ones, altering your life, perspective, and personality. The following statement from a Psalm connects prayer for healing to fasting and sackcloth.

"But as for me, when they were sick my clothing was sackcloth; I humbled my soul with fasting, and my prayer returned unto mine own bosom." (Psalm 35:13)

I'll mention Elijah's words again. I am not better than my fathers. This practice yielded results then, so I believe it yields results now.

OTHER PEOPLE

People can create a great deal of grief. They can be cruel, controlling, abusive, and disruptive. Sometimes, trying to get along with your own family is the most challenging aspect of life. As a side note, our society often proclaims that 'Love Always Wins' and preaches tolerance and acceptance for everyone and everything (or else!). Ironically, the same people get divorced at an alarming rate. If you struggle to get along with your spouse, the one you vetted and selected, then maybe your expectations of general society's ability to show love and tolerance may be unrealistic.

In the Bible, many examples depict people causing hardship for others. Just like Ezra, Nehemiah lived in the generation after the destruction of Jerusalem and took on the responsibility of rebuilding its wall. Among them were individuals determined to disrupt their work, even resorting to assassination attempts.

Presently, Christians in America might not fear for their lives, but in many parts of the world, openly labeling oneself as a Christian can be mortally dangerous. Most of our world lacks freedom and religious liberty. God commands us to behave as Christians. We are not to execute vengeance. Rather, God instructs us to await His justice. In dire situations, our prayer requests become urgent pleas that would benefit from fasting and sackcloth.

"Save me, O God, for the waters have come in unto my soul. I sink into deep mire where there is no standing; I have come into deep waters where the floods overflow me. I am weary of my crying, my throat is dry; mine eyes fail while I wait for my God.

They that hate me without a cause are more than the hairs of mine head; they that would destroy me, being mine enemies wrongfully, are mighty. Then I was made to restore that which I took not away. I have become a stranger unto my brethren, and an alien unto my mother's children. When I wept and chastened my soul with fasting, that was turned to my reproach. I also made sackcloth my garment, and I became a proverb to them. They that sit at the gate speak against me, and I have become the song of the drunkards.

But as for me, my prayer is unto Thee: O Lord, in an acceptable time, O God, in the multitude of Thy mercy hear me in the truth of Thy salvation." (Psalm 69:1-4,8,10-13)

TO GAIN WISDOM AND UNDERSTANDING

Sometimes, in life, you need direction—where to go, what to do, and how to do it. This often involves specific requests for unique circumstances, distinct from the generalized 'God's Will for my life' prayer request that is all too common.

Perhaps you seek a better understanding of God's word, a desire for wisdom, and the request for knowledge. One of God's promises is wisdom, granted to those who ask in unwavering faith (James 1:5-7).

Daniel, too, prayed for wisdom and understanding. In Daniel Chapter 2, there is an account of a time when King Nebuchadnezzar of Babylon had a nightmare. The problem was that he had forgotten the dream but remained disturbed by it. This led him to demand that his wise men, magicians, astrologers, and sorcerers not only remind him of the dream, but also provide its interpretation. However, the King's counselors pushed back, informing Nebuchadnezzar that his request was impossible to fulfill. This enraged the king, who then ordered the execution of all the wise men of Babylon, including Daniel.

Upon hearing this news, Daniel approached the king and requested some time. If granted, he promised to provide both the details of the dream and its interpretation. Nebuchadnezzar temporarily stayed the executions. After returning home, Daniel shared the situation with his three friends, and they prayed. The urgency of the request left no time for fasting. That very night, God revealed the dream and its interpretation to Daniel in a night vision.

In a prayer of gratitude, Daniel recorded:

"Daniel answered and said, 'Blessed be the name of God for ever and ever, for wisdom and might are His. And He changeth the times and the seasons; He removeth kings and setteth up kings. He giveth wisdom unto the wise, and knowledge to them that know understanding. He revealeth the deep and secret things; He knoweth what is in the darkness, and the light dwelleth with Him. I thank Thee and praise Thee, O Thou God of my fathers, who hast given me wisdom and might, and hast made known unto me now what we desired of Thee; for Thou hast now made known unto us the king's matter.'" (Daniel 2:20-23)

Daniel proclaims the truth that God gives wisdom to the wise and knowledge to those that understand it. It is God who reveals deep and secret things. When faced with life-altering decisions or perplexing problems, turning to prayer for wisdom and understanding is an excellent starting point. When you have the wisdom to see things clearly, then decision-making becomes easier.

A friend of mine once shared that he wakes up each day and asks God for wisdom. As I've observed his life's trajectory over the two decades I've known him, it appears, as a casual observer, that God has granted his request. This man consistently seems to stay one step ahead of his peers and repeatedly overcomes difficult situations.

FOR THE NATION

The Bible recounts Daniel engaged in daily prayer, but on certain occasions, he took it a step further by fasting and wearing sackcloth. On one occasion, while he was reading the prophecies of Jeremiah pertaining to Jerusalem, he came across a reference to a 70-year period during which Jerusalem would lie desolate. Touched by this revelation, Daniel prayed for the forgiveness of the Jewish people and the restoration of their nation.

A.S.K.

"In the first year of Darius the son of Ahasuerus, of the seed of the Medes, who was made king over the realm of the Chaldeans, in the first year of his reign I, Daniel, came to understand by books the number of the years, according to the word of the Lord as it came to Jeremiah the prophet, that He would spend seventy years in the desolations of Jerusalem. And I set my face unto the Lord God, seeking by prayer and supplications, with fasting, and sackcloth, and ashes." (Daniel 9:1-3)

The prayer of Daniel is fascinating. He referenced sixteen scriptures from six books in his brief prayer. He was relying on God's word to form his prayer and make his request. Daniel was praying God's will. As Daniel prayed, an angel appeared and said, 'I have now come forth to give thee skill and understanding,' and delivered another prophecy regarding the Jews, which Daniel recorded (Daniel 9:22).

I invite you to read Daniel Chapter 9 in its entirety. For the scholars in our midst, here is the list of the sixteen references to God's written word that Daniel used to form his prayer:

Deuteronomy 7:9, Psalm 106:6, Psalm 119:4,
Jeremiah 25:4, Jeremiah 3:25, Jeremiah 29:18,
Jeremiah 7:19, Psalm 86:5, Deuteronomy 28:15+,
Deuteronomy 30:1-3, Leviticus 22:33, Psalm 71:2,
Psalm 79:4, I Kings 8:29, Psalm 17:6
II Samuel 7:21.

"And this is the confidence that we have in Him: that if we ask anything according to His will, He heareth us." (I John 5:14)

OUR TIME AGAIN

You might wonder if I've put these ideas into practice for myself. The answer is an unequivocal 'yes.' After all, I wouldn't be writing if I hadn't.

Over the past decade, one realization has dawned on me—perhaps we don't pray big enough prayers. As Christians, we all share the desire to witness positive change in the world. That got me thinking. Perhaps we never see significant changes because we never pray big prayers. I suspect that if Christians pray, our prayers are modest, directed primarily towards those in our immediate sphere of influence. When I hear prayers for our nation or the world, they often lack specificity, making it a challenge to discern God's response. After all, if you don't pray for a precise outcome and only pray in generalities, how do you determine whether God granted your request?

The following example, along with two others I'll later explain, hopefully will provoke some thought. My desire is to communicate the details in a way that motivates you to experiment on your own. I have no intention of elevating myself as a religious figure; I'm an ordinary man living an ordinary life. As I recount my experiences with three big prayers and their subsequent outcomes, it's plausible for a skeptic to suggest that I might exhibit confirmation bias — a person's tendency to process information by looking for, or interpreting, information that is consistent with their existing beliefs. However, the three occasions on which I prayed big seem to transcend mere coincidence.

I typically avoid referencing current events in my writing because historical details fade with time, potentially diluting the message I aim to convey. For context, it's worth noting that I am writing this book in the fall of 2023, and the big prayer I'm about to describe transpired in early 2016.

During this period in America, the signs of societal decay had become increasingly apparent. Newspapers filled their pages with scandals of all sorts, and government corruption, although sporadically exposed, appeared to infect multiple levels of governance. This was vexing my soul. Why? Because I knew nothing good could ever come from this corruption, and eventually, the repercussions of this decay would reach even my doorstep, so to speak.

So, I asked myself, "How long will this continue? When will God judge?". It was a prayer that felt deserving of fasting, sackcloth, and ashes. I asked God, perhaps even begged, for change. My plan was to ask God to expose the corruption, shine the light on the evil deeds of man, and root it out.

A.S.K.

In my mind, I envisioned entering the courtroom and standing before the Divine Judge. I took weeks to ponder my request and form my prayer. I developed the reasons God should respond to my prayer, and I searched for other instances in the Bible that mirrored the circumstances. And then, I began a period of fasting. I fasted for three days initially, followed by two days twice over, totaling seven days. There was even a day when I sat in sackcloth and ashes because my soul was vexed. My prayer contained several verses and thoughts.

"O Lord, how long shall I cry, and Thou wilt not hear? Even cry out unto Thee of violence, and Thou wilt not save? Why dost Thou show me iniquity, and cause me to behold grievance? For despoiling and violence are before me, and there are those that raise up strife and contention. Therefore the law is slacked, and judgment doth never go forth. For the wicked doth compass about the righteous; therefore wrong judgment proceedeth." (Habakkuk 1:2-4)

These verses were a perfect encapsulation in America in early 2016. Everywhere I looked, people despised God's word and His ways. Marriages and families were breaking apart. Sexual perversion was growing exponentially. Government corruption and injustice abounded. Hardcore drugs were being legalized. People actively destroyed themselves through vice. Christian social-drinkers were consuming copious amounts of alcohol and ignoring God's wisdom that sobriety is our goal.

Jeremiah's writing matched the state of the nation.

"For among My people are found wicked men; they lie in wait as he that setteth snares; they set a trap, they catch men. As a cage is full of birds, so are their houses full of deceit; therefore they have become great and have waxed rich. They have waxed fat, they shine; yea, they surpass the deeds of the wicked; they judge not the cause, the cause of the fatherless, yet they prosper; and the right of the needy do they not judge.

'Shall I not visit for these things?' saith the Lord. 'Shall not My soul be avenged on such a nation as this? An astonishing and horrible thing is committed in the land: The prophets prophesy falsely, and the priests bear rule by their means; and My people love to have it so. And what will ye do in the end thereof?'" (Jeremiah 5:26-31)

The statement, "my people love to have it so" really stands out. I don't know many people, but the ones that I know don't seem to care. The pursuits of pleasure are the primary motivators. Perhaps I'm too critical, but that's how I'm seeing it. What am I to do? If I were to make a change myself, it would be futile. A small firecracker tossed into a hurricane. I am a simple man. One person in some backwoods town in the center of Pennsylvania. I am nobody. Without clout, pull or significance. What the Bible says will be true of me. I won't leave a lasting memory beyond my time on this earth. Any remembrance will fade into darkness soon. I have no strength and there is nothing I can do.

But I know something important, and I know someone important. The LORD spoke words, and the universe sprang into existence. God declared the strength of his arm and the power of his might. God can make a change without breaking a sweat. I know that without God's involvement, there is no hope.

I took these thoughts and Bible verses, formulated my prayer wrapped in fasting and sackcloth. I asked for a change in our government, in our homes, in our churches, in our nation, in our world. It was a big request.

Keep in mind that this prayer was the spring of 2016. I'm writing in 2023. Has anything big happened in the intervening seven years?

Without a doubt. There are too many things to count. It's almost like the news cycle is now on steroids. I'll spend a few moments recalling the highlights to catch you up on history. An outsider defeated a highly favored presidential candidate. Politics corrupted law enforcement. Several highly respected sexual predators were unmasked. A perverted island used for trafficking the young to the rich and powerful is no longer in use. People now widely regard the media as propagandist and liars. Two impeachments of a sitting president. Someone unleashed a man-enhanced virus causing worldwide disruptions and death. The problem of a vaccine with unknown long-term side effects is becoming a concern for many. There is increasing scrutiny of the business practices of pharmaceutical companies. The censoring of free speech is being exposed and litigated. Other government abuses of power are coming to light. The negative effects of social media are getting noticed. Many natural disasters receive the 'unprecedented' label. Hedonism receives praise in every facet of our culture. Wars and rumors of wars are rampant. Talk of nuclear war is normal again. Violence and hatred rule in our streets. Scientists are being exposed for sacrificing the pursuit of truth in favor of grant money and notoriety. America's grip on world power is slipping. The world's economy is under duress. People view elections as untrustworthy, regardless of their politics or country. Every pillar of society and culture are being shaken. Even the church, Protestant and Catholic alike, are showing fractures and divisions.

Did God answer my prayer? It seems like things are transforming. Was this because of my prayer? I have no way of knowing. The prayer is big, and the world's systems are complex. I don't have a way of knowing everything that happens because I have no access to the data points. I prayed for the US government's corruption to be exposed, and that has happened, and continues to happen. Was it because of my prayer? Who knows? I do not know if there was only my one prayer, or if perhaps millions of God's people were offering similar requests and He's responded to all of us.

You can think about this yourself, but it seems there is a struggle in our world that didn't exist before. It's like there's an old fashion western showdown coming to a head. Wicked strongholds don't like disruption. I think there are more dramatic events on the horizon and the proverbial storm-clouds are gathering. If God is moving, He isn't done.

I could go on, but historical events get lost in context. Many authors have written books about the events of the past 7 years. However, these books only touch the surface of the rapid change.

One pillar of the Christian faith is hope, and my attempts at praying big give me hope for the future. The best is still yet to come. There is more to existence than this life. I don't know if anything I've done, prayers I've uttered, and the labor I'm putting into this book will have any impact. All my efforts might amount to nothing, but then again, maybe they are more important than I can imagine. I can't wait to find out, and that excitement for the future, where I will learn how it all fits together, including my small part, offers me hope.

Meanwhile, I often like to know if I'm on the right track with my prayer requests. For this first attempt at praying big, I added a little request for a sign, a fleece if you will, to see if this prayer was going anywhere. And boy, did I get a surprise.

A.S.K.

4

Decisions

4

Decisions

Life is complex, and we often face hard choices. It's like navigating the fog of war.

So, let's consider a scenario where you require specific guidance for an impending choice—a situation distinct from the broader concept of 'God's will for your life.' How do you make these decisions effectively? Do you rely on intuition, a systematic, analytical approach, seeking counsel from friends and family, or perhaps even procrastinating, hoping the situation resolves itself?

I suspect many individuals employ varying methods based on the circumstances at hand. However, I believe that seeking God's guidance is the most successful approach. To elaborate on this notion, let us turn our attention to how the Bible characterizes itself, paying particular attention to the term 'profitable'.

"But continue thou in the things which thou hast learned and hast been assured of, knowing from whom thou hast learned them, and that from childhood thou hast known the Holy Scriptures, which are able to make thee wise unto salvation through faith which is in Christ Jesus. All Scripture is given by inspiration of God and is profitable for doctrine, for reproof, for correction, for instruction in righteousness, that the man of God may be perfect, thoroughly equipped for all good works." (II Timothy 3:14-17)

Some people study the Bible for academic reasons, but I find value in understanding how it applies to our daily lives. The Bible itself asserts that one of its advantages is providing 'instruction in righteousness'. It encourages us to apply its teachings to our lifestyles and habits, guiding us toward perfection and preparing us for all good works. If we appropriately apply the lessons of the Bible, when life's storms rage, our foundation remains unshaken, firmly rooted in the rock.

When the Apostle Paul penned this letter to Timothy, the New Testament had yet to be compiled; only the Old Testament existed. Therefore, when you read this passage, you recognize Timothy knew the 'holy scriptures' of the Old Testament from his childhood. The Apostle Paul declares that within the pages of the Old Testament lies the wisdom that can lead one to salvation through faith in Christ Jesus. The Old Testament contains divine inspiration and offers teachings that are profitable for doctrine, rebuke, correction, and instruction in righteousness.

The same applies to the New Testament. We should embrace the Old Testament as much as the New Testament. Its volume is about three times that of the New Testament, offering a wealth of lessons to consider. I'm not advocating for a return to the Mosaic Law. Broadly speaking, the Law encompassed three aspects: civil law, religious law, and moral law. The civil and religious laws were specific to governing the religious society and government of the Israelites, while the moral law remains unchanging. Even as Christians, the moral law serves as a steadfast foundation for guidance in righteousness.

If you seek direction in your life or require help with challenging decisions, the Bible offers help and hope. The Old Testament holds many valuable lessons. It combines proverbs, prayers, prophecies, commandments, songs of praise, and historical narratives detailing human behavior and God's responses. These stories offer unvarnished truths and reveal the imperfections of even the most esteemed individuals. Consider, for instance, the valuable lesson provided in the following verse.

"In all thy ways acknowledge Him, and He shall direct thy paths." (Proverbs 3:6)

God extends a grand bargain. If you acknowledge Him, He promises to direct your path. I compare it to a child's experience in a bowling alley, where they place bumpers in the lane gutters to ensure the bowling ball stays on course and never falls into the gutter. In life, if you acknowledge God, God provides the 'bumpers' to keep you out of the gutter, and on the path moving towards the goal.

So, how do you acknowledge God? The method may not have a one-size-fits all formula. However, I think cultivating a daily habit of reading the Bible is a significant starting point. It signifies your recognition of God's Word and your eagerness to understand His guidance. Recently, I've adopted a habit of thanking God at the end of each day for at least one thing, inspired by Brian Sussman's recommendation (he's famous, look him up). My dog often gets a mention in my prayers, as she finds it quite enjoyable when I kneel on the floor for prayer. In the morning, I thank God for being alive and the sense that all my bodily functions appear to be normal.

When faced with a big decision, acknowledging God involves actively seeking His guidance, earnestly seeking answers from Him on how best to proceed. The Bible offers many examples of people seeking divine guidance for hard choices, which I use as my 'legal precedent' to help guide my requests.

It's important to note that the Bible provides established guidelines, and for these areas, you don't need to seek additional guidance. The Bible has already provided the 'instruction in righteousness'. For instance, if you're a Christian contemplating marriage to a non-believer, the Bible establishes its direction: the answer is no.

> "Be ye not unequally yoked together with unbelievers, for what fellowship hath righteousness with unrighteousness? And what communion hath light with darkness?" (II Corinthians 6:14)

If you become a believer after your marriage, and your spouse is a non-believer, then you should stay married.

> "But to the rest I speak (not the Lord): if any brother hath a wife who believeth not, and she be pleased to dwell with him, let him not put her away. And the woman who hath a husband who

believeth not, and if he be pleased to dwell with her, let her not leave him." (I Corinthians 7:12-13)

If you are contemplating entering a business partnership with an unbeliever, the answer is no.

"Blessed is the man that walketh not in the counsel of the ungodly, nor standeth in the way of sinners, nor sitteth in the seat of the scornful;" (Psalm 1:1)

During the midst of an economic crisis, a woman asked for prayer on whether to abandon her home mortgage. Again, this does not need prayer because the Bible has already provided guidance.

"The wicked borroweth, and payeth not again:" (Psalm 37:21)

The Bible contains guidance on a multitude of matters, which I consider being 'God's will for your life'. They are explicit commands we should follow.

However, not all decisions in life come with obvious answers. The diversity of human experience across millennia is so varied that it would be impossible to write a manual detailing the choice for every circumstance. In these situations, I turn to the concept of 'fleeces', an idea from a story in the Book of Judges involving a man named Gideon. I have found this example to be a valuable basis for successfully experimenting with decision-making in my life.

Please note that some criticize 'fleeces' as a sign of lacking faith. I think the story of Gideon illustrates the exact opposite. Please give me a moment to explain, starting with the following verse.

"Thus saith the Lord: 'Stand ye in the highways and see, and ask for the old paths, where is the good way; and walk therein, and ye shall find rest for your souls.'" (Jeremiah 6:16)

A.S.K.

I love this verse. The LORD offers rest for your soul, but it requires your active participation. The rest for your soul will come by pausing the busyness of your life, looking around, and then comparing what you see with the old paths found in the Bible. Once you've become familiar with these 'old paths' described as the 'good way', and actively walk in them by following the Bible's instructions, you will find rest for your soul.

The concept of a 'fleece' is one of these old paths. After all, it worked then. Why not now?

During Gideon's generation, the Israelites found themselves in a predicament because they strayed from the old path and departed from God's instructions.

"And the children of Israel did evil in the sight of the Lord, and the Lord delivered them into the hand of Midian seven years. And Israel was greatly impoverished because of the Midianites, and the children of Israel cried unto the Lord." (Judges 6:1,6)

I had a pastor who often said, "If you can't listen, then you can feel." This is a perfect summary of a fundamental truth. You can choose to heed God's Word and follow the 'old path', or you can ignore those paths and feel the pain of the consequences.

With the Israelites, their refusal to listen led them to endure the painful consequences of oppression and impoverishment for seven years. However, the Israelites finally did the right thing and cried out to the Lord. He responded.

"And there came an angel of the Lord, and sat under an oak which was in Ophrah, that pertained unto Joash the Abiezrite; and his son Gideon threshed wheat by the wine press to hide it from the Midianites. And the angel of the Lord appeared unto him and said unto him, 'The Lord is with thee, thou mighty man of valor.'
And Gideon said unto him, 'Oh my lord, if the Lord be with us, why then has all this befallen us? And where are all His miracles

which our fathers told us of, saying, 'Did not the Lord bring us up from Egypt?' But now the Lord hath forsaken us and delivered us into the hands of the Midianites."' (Judges 6:11-13)

Gideon, unlike those who had witnessed the miracles of the Exodus from Egypt, had not experienced such wonders. Instead, he lived in a society marked by decay and facing the consequences of its decline.

"And the Lord looked upon him, and said, 'Go in this thy might, and thou shalt save Israel from the hand of the Midianites. Have not I sent thee?'
And he said unto Him, 'Oh my Lord, with what shall I save Israel? Behold, my family is poor in Manasseh, and I am the least in my father's house.'
And the Lord said unto him, 'Surely I will be with thee, and thou shalt smite the Midianites as one man.'
And he said unto Him, 'If now I have found grace in Thy sight, then show me a sign that Thou talkest with me.'" (Judges 6:14-17)

I think attitude matters. Consider Gideon's request for a sign—he exemplified a humble attitude. He didn't demand a sign or exhibit the skepticism of a 'doubting Thomas' who required tangible proof. Instead, Gideon approached God with a humble plea, seeking His grace to confirm that it was indeed the Lord speaking. It's not an unreasonable request. When God spoke with Moses through the bush that remained unconsumed by fire, Moses had visual evidence of God's presence before their conversation began.

In Gideon's situation, he encountered an apparently ordinary individual delivering divine directives as if he were God. It's only natural for a rational person to exercise caution when accepting a stranger's proclamations. Gideon had faith. He believed in the God of Israel and believed God occasionally visited His people, Israel. So, he humbly asked for God's grace and support. Gideon further specified his request for a sign, and it's worth noting the simplicity of Gideon's ask: 'Stay here until I can prepare a meal for you.'

A.S.K.

It might seem like a strange request. After all, what can a meal prove? My observation is that Gideon understood spiritual beings do not eat physical food. Therefore, if this individual consumed a meal, it would show they were a normal person, not an angelic being. Following His resurrection, Jesus deliberately ate with His disciples to prove His physical resurrection and dispel any notion that He was a ghost. Gideon was smart; his meal request served as a litmus test, and it worked.

"'Depart not hence, I pray Thee, until I come unto Thee and bring forth my present and set it before Thee.'

And He said, 'I will tarry until thou come again.'

And Gideon went in, and made ready a kid and unleavened cakes of an ephah of flour. The flesh he put in a basket, and he put the broth in a pot, and brought it out unto him under the oak and presented it.

And the angel of God said unto him, 'Take the flesh and the unleavened cakes, and lay them upon this rock, and pour out the broth.' And he did so.

Then the angel of the Lord put forth the end of the staff that was in his hand, and touched the flesh and the unleavened cakes; and there rose up fire out of the rock, and consumed the flesh and the unleavened cakes. Then the angel of the Lord departed out of his sight. And when Gideon perceived that he was an angel of the Lord, Gideon said, 'Alas, O Lord God! For I have seen an angel of the Lord face to face.'" (Judges 6:18-22)

God understands our failings. He knows we need encouragement and help along our way. Gideon does not differ from any of us. He needed a confidence boost to set things in motion. This initial encounter with the angel of the Lord started a movement that would ultimately liberate Israel from their oppressors. It all began that very night; Gideon found his courage.

"And it came to pass the same night, that the Lord said unto him, 'Take thy father's young bullock, even the second bullock of seven years old, and throw down the altar of Baal that thy father hath, and cut down the Asherah pole that is by it; and build an altar unto the Lord thy God upon the top of this rock in the ordered place, and take the second bullock and offer a burnt sacrifice with the wood of the Asherah pole which thou shalt cut down.'

Then Gideon took ten men of his servants and did as the Lord had said unto him. And so it was, because he feared his father's household and the men of the city, that he could not do it by day, so that he did it by night." (Judges 6:25-27)

The destruction of Baal's altar posed a significant level of mortal danger for Gideon. Gideon was, in fact, committing a capital offense, and the Baal worshippers would readily seek his execution for what they considered blasphemy. As the saying goes, 'loose lips sink ships', and Gideon had no less than ten witnesses who might betray him—unfortunately, one of them did. Regardless of the risk, Gideon found the courage to take this perilous action because of the miraculous display of God's power earlier in the day.

After they discovered Gideon's clandestine act, and he became implicated in the 'crime', Gideon's father stepped in and used clever sarcasm to defuse the angry crowd.

"And when the men of the city arose early in the morning, behold, the altar of Baal was cast down and the Asherah pole was cut down that was by it, and the second bullock was offered upon the altar that was built. And they said one to another, 'Who hath done this thing?'

And when they inquired and asked, they said, 'Gideon the son of Joash hath done this thing.'

Then the men of the city said unto Joash, 'Bring out thy son, that he may die, because he hath cast down the altar of Baal and because he hath cut down the Asherah pole that was by it.'

And Joash said unto all who stood against him, 'Will ye plead for Baal? Will ye save him? He that will plead for him, let him be put to death whilst it is yet morning. If he be a god, let him plead

A.S.K.

for himself, because one hath cast down his altar.'" (Judges 6:28-31)

What an ingenious response to an angry crowd! Gideon's father put the faith of the Baal worshippers to the test by challenging them, suggesting that if Baal is indeed a god, then let Baal avenge himself. Subsequently, these men were too ashamed to take justice into their own hands. From that day onward, they referred to Gideon as Jerubbaal, saying, 'Let Baal plead against him, because he has thrown down his altar.'

As had been the tradition in previous years, the Midianites, the Amalekites, and the children of the East assembled in the Valley of Jezreel to begin their annual pillaging of Israel. The Bible describes the multitude as numerous as grasshoppers blanketing the land. However, this year was different; God's Spirit moved Gideon to rally an army bent on rebellion.

Gideon received his initial sign from the angel, which spurred him to risk his life to follow God's command. Subsequently, Gideon felt the stirrings of God's Spirit within, leading him to gather an army. However, the next course of action remained uncertain.

You may have heard the story of Gideon, and if so, then you are aware of the eventual outcome. However, I invite you to take a moment to put yourself in this situation. Imagine you are in immediate peril of certain death, a result of overwhelming odds, which are weighing heavily on your mind. You have a divine mandate demanding you to act, but what is your next step? Would you think it prudent to proceed with a well-crafted battle plan, knowing that failure could lead to your demise? Or, given the stakes, would you seek divine guidance?

Let us assume that you have recently encountered an angel who bolstered your spirits with a miraculous sign. Considering this extraordinary encounter with the supernatural, would you feel inclined to seek further interaction with the divine realm?

If you are truly being honest and can imagine yourself in this perilous situation, with your life hanging in the balance and the outcome unknown, the only logical conclusion is 'yes'. You would earnestly seek God's approval before proceeding.

At this point in the story, Gideon was far from knowing how it would end. He was living it moment by moment, and faced with such uncertainty, he turned to God for a second sign. Many argue that Gideon's request signified a lack of faith, but I hold a different perspective. Gideon's actions at this stage reflect a collaborative interaction with God. Without faith, Gideon would not have asked for another miracle. To request such a divine intervention, one must first have faith in God's power. Seeking God is a testament to faith, not a sign of its absence.

If you still believe that Gideon's request for a second sign was inappropriate, then what should Gideon have done differently? Should Gideon have opted for an immediate attack with his army? Sought additional armed support from neighboring nations? Proposed peace with his oppressors? Or procrastinated until the events unfolded? I pose these questions sincerely; I am not being sarcastic. What course of action could have been superior to seeking God's counsel, especially when it had recently resulted in a positive outcome through his encounter with the angel?

The fundamental lesson is the process of actively seeking God. Gideon believed God, yet he sought assurance that he was following the right path and had divine approval to proceed. The urgency of the situation demanded a swift decision. The Bible itself notes that 'the Spirit of the Lord came upon Gideon' (Judges 6:34), suggesting that Gideon may have acted under the influence or guidance of the Spirit of the Lord in his actions. I think it's a thoughtful question to consider: Did the origins of the idea for the second sign stem from Gideon's own mind, or was it inspired by the Spirit?

Another critical aspect to consider is the far-reaching consequences of Gideon's rebellion, which would affect all of Israel. The result, good or bad, wasn't his alone to bear. His army's lives were at stake, and the rest of Israel, including women and children, would suffer the vengeance of the enemy if the rebellion failed. This was a serious time, with no room for error.

Israel's history might have played a part in Gideon's need for certainty regarding God's approval. Surely, he was aware of the past accounts of Israelites who ventured into battle without God's blessing, leading to their failures, such as the initial attempt to claim the promised land or the battle of Ai. History had shown that attempting to engage in warfare without God's guidance resulted in catastrophic outcomes for the Israelites.

Gideon held a solemn duty to both his army and his nation. His responsibility was to proceed only if he could secure God's guarantee of victory.

A.S.K.

It required faith to find oneself in a time-crunch situation, seek God's direction, and exercise the patience to await a divine response.

It's easy to sit in the comfort of a pew in America and pass judgment, claiming that Gideon lacked faith. This perspective is misguided. Put yourself in his shoes. If you found yourself in a similar circumstance, it would be wise to seek God's counsel. The stakes are too high for everyone involved.

Fortunately, you rarely grapple with life-or-death decisions. However, this doesn't mean that you should simply pursue your best formed plans. I believe God invites us to inquire of him. Jesus proclaimed in Luke 11:9-10: "And I say unto you: ask, and it shall be given you; seek, and ye shall find; knock, and it shall be opened unto you. For every one that asketh receiveth, and he that seeketh findeth, and to him that knocketh it shall be opened." God welcomes our inquiries.

Gideon, through faith, sought God's approval to proceed with the rebellion. Gideon requested a miraculous sign involving a fleece of wool. This choice gave rise to the concept of a 'prayer fleece.' While God's angel had declared that Gideon would smite the Midianites as one man, the precise 'how' and 'when' remained unclear. Gideon, in an act of faith, prayed for a miraculous sign, an experiment if you will, to confirm God's timing and the success of his rebellion.

"And Gideon said unto God, 'If Thou wilt save Israel by mine hand, as Thou hast said—behold, I will put a fleece of wool on the floor; and if the dew be on the fleece only, and it be dry upon all the earth beside, then shall I know that Thou wilt save Israel by mine hand, as Thou hast said.'
And it was so; for he rose up early on the morrow, and thrust the fleece together, and wrung the dew out of the fleece, a bowl full of water." (Judges 6:36-38)

Gideon didn't stop at just one request; he took it a step further and asked for the opposite. Notice the humility in his request. Gideon knew he was pushing the boundaries a little with his additional inquiry, yet he asked anyway.

"And Gideon said unto God, 'Let not Thine anger be hot against me, and I will speak but this once. Let me prove, I pray Thee, but this once with the fleece: Let it now be dry only upon the fleece, and upon all the ground let there be dew.'

And God did so that night; for it was dry upon the fleece only, and there was dew on all the ground." (Judges 6:39-40)

If you have been keeping count, you'll notice that God provided assurance to Gideon on four different occasions. What's significant is that there isn't a single indication in God's Word that He frowned upon Gideon's behavior. God has since elevated Gideon within His Word as a model of courage and faith. Hebrews chapter 11, often referred to as the 'faith hall of fame', mentions Gideon for his faith. It bothers me to hear someone proclaim that Gideon lacked faith when God's own words never condemned his actions. Therefore, I interpret Gideon's story as an invitation to learn how to approach God and apply this knowledge to our own lives. Gideon's experience has now become one of the 'old paths.'

It's crucial to recall that the Midianites oppressed Gideon and his people, causing them to endure seven years of hardship and suffering. They were all poor. The Midianites stole nearly everything they produced. There was no organized or trained army; Gideon and his countrymen spent the years hiding in dens and caves. To lead a rebellion against overwhelming odds in such dire circumstances requires an immense faith in God.

God's goal was to remind Israel that He is the one and only God and to prove to the surrounding nations the futility of their false idols. To make His power known, God decided to 'up the ante'. God tasked Gideon with something counterintuitive, to reduce the size of his pathetic army.

"And the Lord said unto Gideon, 'The people who are with thee are too many for Me to give the Midianites into their hands, lest Israel vaunt themselves against Me, saying, 'Mine own hand hath saved me.'" (Judges 7:2)

To reduce the size of the army, God instructed Gideon to dismiss anyone who was afraid to fight. As a result, 22,000 men left, leaving just 10,000 men.

A.S.K.

However, even with 10,000 men, God considered it too many. He provided Gideon with another instruction; have the men drink from water. Only those men who lapped the water like a dog by putting their hand to their mouth could stay. In the end, only 300 men remained.

God then proclaimed that these 300 men would be the instrument of victory against the multitude of Midianites, who covered the land like a swarm of grasshoppers.

Here is an intriguing part of the story. Did Gideon ask for another 'fleece?' No, he does not. Does God provide another 'fleece?' Why yes, He does, even without asking!

God was ready to work. He inspired Gideon through the Spirit of the Lord, demonstrated His support four times, and yet freely offered another situation to reinforce Gideon's faith.

"And it came to pass the same night that the Lord said unto him, 'Arise, get thee down unto the host, for I have delivered it into thine hand. But if thou fear to go down, go thou with Purah thy servant down to the host, and thou shalt hear what they say; and afterward shall thine hands be strengthened to go down unto the host.'
Then went he down with Purah his servant unto the outside of the armed men who were in the host." (Judges 7:9-11)

God understood the circumstance and easily recognized the anxiety that Gideon was feeling (who wouldn't be anxious in such a situation) and extended further comfort through a fifth sign.

"And the Midianites and the Amalekites and all the children of the East lay along in the valley like grasshoppers for multitude; and their camels were without number, as the sand by the seaside for multitude.

And when Gideon had come, behold, there was a man who told a dream unto his fellow, and said, 'Behold, I dreamed a dream; and lo, a cake of barley bread tumbled into the host of Midian and came unto a tent, and smote it so that it fell, and overturned it so that the tent lay flat.'

And his fellow answered and said, 'This is nothing else save the sword of Gideon the son of Joash, a man of Israel, for into his hand hath God delivered Midian and all the host.'

And it was so, when Gideon heard the telling of the dream and the interpretation thereof, that he worshipped, and returned into the host of Israel and said, 'Arise, for the Lord hath delivered into your hand the host of Midian.'" (Judges 7:12-15)

Isn't this a magnificent story? It portrays the intricate interplay between God and man during a profoundly distressing time. Gideon's inquiries, his asking, seeking, knocking, and ultimately his faith put into action through obedience to God all contributed to this inspiring story. God responded at each step of the way with no criticism directed towards Gideon.

You can read the details of God's miracle in Judges 7. The victory was so complete that the Midianites never recovered. And I mean never recovered. They no longer exist as an identifiable group of people.

"Thus was Midian subdued before the children of Israel, so that they lifted up their heads no more. And the country was in quietness forty years in the days of Gideon." (Judges 8:28)

EXPERIENCE, NOT ACADEMICS

I know 'prayer fleeces' are effective because I've tried it many times, with outstanding success. At no point did I ever feel as though I was overstepping my boundaries, nor did I experience any pangs of guilt within my conscience. My exploration of this practice started with smaller, less critical matters and then progressed to significant decisions. Rarely do I make impactful choices without first employing this strategy, hoping to gain insight into God's preferred path.

Through this ongoing process, as I've witnessed firsthand the results and guidance it provides, my faith has continued to grow. It's sort of like lifting weights—beginning with small weights until they become too easy and then exercising with heavier barbells. The same is true of faith. Starting small and learning will strengthen your faith until eventually you'll be able to carry heavy loads—and without doubt.

I often think I should compile a history of my experiences instead of relying on memory. Even the most amazing answers to prayer fade from memory over time, which is why reading the Bible daily helps remind me of the greatness of God. In the following sections, I'll explain a few of my many experiments, provide additional examples from the Bible, and share experiences of others to illustrate that I am not unique.

THE PRAYER BOX

For several years, I taught Sunday school to a group of young adults aged 18-23. Initially, preparing lessons was a real chore. Each week, I would labor over commentaries and other resources, hoping to present the Bible effectively. It was a terrible process, and my lessons were dreadful. This continued for about four years. The root of the problem was that I didn't know my Bible. I rarely read it.

I know, I know—it seems silly that I was teaching the Bible without being a regular reader, but I had grown up in the church, and I had developed a sense of familiarity with its contents. However, my knowledge was superficial at best. Although I was familiar with many of the prominent stories, I didn't truly comprehend the full scope of the Bible or its teachings.

Then, in the year 2000, I made a pivotal decision. I purchased a Reese Chronological Bible and committed myself to reading it once a year. The things I learned in that first reading opened my eyes to an entirely new world within the Bible. I soon read it more than once a year, and my reading habits sped up from there. Guess what happened? I no longer struggled to prepare Sunday school lessons. I was learning so much by simply reading that by the time each Sunday arrived, I could deliver a lesson founded on the ideas and knowledge I had gained directly from the Bible itself. It was like a fountain that never ran dry.

I noticed a positive shift in my students' engagement as well. Instead of regurgitating a commentary or someone else's material, I could present lessons fresh from the pages of the Bible.

All the while, my faith was growing. I experienced what the Bible explained in rather simple terms, but something I had failed to understand for decades.

"So then faith cometh by hearing, and hearing by the Word of God." (Romans 10:17)

Your faith can grow, but there is a process. The best way to understand this verse is to reverse the statement. Here is how I would put it: The Word of God leads to hearing from God, which increases your faith. This is the truth. If you read the Bible, eventually God's Word will cause you to think differently, and you'll begin understanding the world around you differently, and God will start communicating with you through His Word and your circumstances.

The lessons from the Word of God will establish roots in your mind and then circumstances you face will reinforce them. Many Christians will testify to the same strange phenomena. Once you experience this dynamic interaction between the Bible, your mind, and your daily occurrences, your faith will grow. It's an inevitable outcome as long as you remain committed to reading the Bible.

After a few years, I began pondering ways to help my Sunday school students grow their faith. After some contemplation, I settled on an idea that I named 'The Prayer Box,' which I presented to my class. The concept was simple: I provided a shoebox with a slot for inserting prayer requests. I encouraged the students to write a prayer on a slip of paper and place it in the prayer box. Each Sunday morning, we'd draw one request at random, pray for that request, and then ask God to answer the prayer by the following Sunday morning.

My logic behind this idea was loosely based on the Old Testament tradition of casting lots. By leaving the choice in God's hands by the randomness of the drawing, God could decide the timing of the prayers He wished to answer. If

A.S.K.

He established a pattern of answered prayers, I believed it would serve as a catalyst for my student's faith to grow.

I gave my students explicit instructions. The goal was to begin with small, specific requests. Each prayer needed to be something small, yet unique enough that, if answered, it would serve as a clear sign of God's involvement. Generalized requests wouldn't be of much use.

I knew this was unorthodox, and I wasn't sure it would work. I felt a little foolish. It would be much easier to maintain a status quo, teach a bland lesson each week, and go home. After all, as the saying goes, 'why rock the boat?' However, I couldn't shake off this idea; it remained in my head, and I felt compelled to find out what would happen. As I explained the concept to my students, they posed questions to clarify the rules. However, I found myself in need of an example they could readily grasp. With no thought, I said the first thing that came to mind that morning of December 6, 2003. The date is significant because of what happened next.

I explained to my students that, for instance, a prayer could be as specific as: 'I pray that the United States captures Saddam Hussein by this time next week.' I explained that it would be solely up to God to determine when that prayer request would get drawn from the box, and it was exceptionally specific, and then we could determine if the prayer received an answer within the week. I was trying to stress the importance of praying for a specific outcome. If you pray in generalities, you will never know if God answered your prayer.

If you have any familiarity with the Saddam Hussein situation, you'd know that the U.S. military had been on a relentless hunt for him since around April 2003, for nearly eight months, with no success in locating him.

Guess what happened? The following Sunday morning, on December 13, 2003, as I was preparing for church, I briefly turned on the national news. To my astonishment, they were pulling Saddam Hussein out of the spider hole in Iraq, where he'd been hiding. It happened just seven days after I had spontaneously provided the example related to the prayer box. I felt dumbfounded. The timing was extraordinarily uncanny. It begged the question: How could this possibly be mere coincidence? I had a multitude of examples I could have provided, nearly an infinite array. And yet, my specific example received validation that very week. It felt like an impossibility.

Did the prayer box prove effective? Yes, it did. Any small, specific prayer would consistently receive an answer by the following week. However, there was a challenge—my students often struggled to provide specific requests. For instance, one wrote, 'I pray I have a wonderful week'. I didn't want to discourage them from participating, so I refrained from criticism. Requests of this nature were no good because they lacked specificity, and the outcome was arbitrary.

Then there were those who aimed for specificity, but a result within one week would be impossible. One student asked for the Detroit Pistons of the National Basketball Association to achieve 50-wins for the 2004-2005 season, which was specific but beyond the one-week turnaround. Incidentally, the Detroit Pistons achieved over 50 wins that season but lost in the Championship round. In a tongue-in-cheek manner, I suggested to the student that he should have asked for a championship because 50 wins, in the grand scheme of things, didn't hold the same weight.

Many other requests failed to be specific, resulting in inconclusive outcomes. Eventually, it became hard to get anyone to submit entries into the prayer box and the experiment ended.

Do I recall any of my students' successful requests and corresponding answers? Unfortunately, I do not. I thought I would remember them all, but now time has fogged my memory. I should have written them down. One request involved a car purchase, while another request involved a friend, but I have lost the precise details. I have learned that part of our failings as humans is our inability to remember. God does amazing things, and we forget. The nation of Israel saw amazing miracles and then forgot.

What I vividly remember is my own specific request and the remarkable answer. I had lost a belt. My prayer request was straightforward: 'God, please help me find my belt.' I placed this request in the prayer box, where it languished for many months without being drawn. When I finally drew my request, to be honest, I thought to myself that this would be a failure. After all, the belt had been missing for approximately six months, and it had vanished without a trace. If it were still in our possession, surely, we would have stumbled upon it at some point.

Later that week, my family and I had a trip planned to visit my in-laws, who lived a seven-hour drive away. After spending a few days with them, we were preparing to depart. I made one last check of the bedroom to ensure we had collected all our belongings. As I was about to leave the bedroom and casting one last glance around, I received that little ping, nudging me to look for my belt behind and underneath a cedar chest along the far wall. I knelt and, to my astonishment, there lay my long-lost belt. The answer was right there. Within that very week. Coincidence? It cannot be.

This is just one of many things I've witnessed. The evidence is clear—God is real. I suspect He delights in surprising us. I also think our prayer requests are often too vague. Without specific requests, how can we truly discern whether God has responded?

All of this brings us back to the notion that when you're forming a request, prepare your reasonings like you would prepare for an earthly judge. What exactly is your request, and why do you seek it? What specific outcome do you desire? An earthly judge would demand to know these details. As you prepare your reasonings and read your Bible, I think God helps you craft the prayer that aligns with His will. Once this happens, the results will follow.

SHOULD I REPLACE MY CAR?

In 2007, I had this old car with nearly 200,000 miles on it. Maybe I'm frugal, but I've always liked to think I'm getting my monies worth. However, I couldn't quite decide whether to replace it. This wasn't exactly a life-or-death situation, but part of my process of acknowledging God was to ask for His opinion.

I prayed about this decision for quite some time, but there were no answers. After months of prayer, I changed my strategy. I formed an updated prayer: "Lord, here's my plan. If it's okay to get another car, then make it very apparent that it's okay. Otherwise, I'm not doing anything. Amen."

I offered this prayer on a Sunday. Four days later, an accident totaled my car.

Is this a coincidence? Before you answer, here are some facts to consider. For over 37 years of driving, this is my one and only accident. Only four days after I offered a 'fleece' type prayer asking for a clear sign to help me make a comfortable decision, an accident occurred which totaled the car. Coincidence? I think not.

There's a lot to this story that makes it unique. First, the accident happened in a parking lot, which isn't where you'd expect to see a car totaled. At the entrance to the parking lot, there was a crossroads, and the other driver was traveling at such a high rate of speed that he broadsided my car right as I entered from the street. However, no one sustained any injuries. The other driver's insurance company matched mine, which allowed the insurance company to waive my deductible.

Normally, the police do not assign fault in parking lot accidents, but in this case, the cause of the accident was so apparent that they assigned the fault to the offending driver. To make the situation somewhat more memorable (maybe even enjoyable), as the police officer was in his car, processing our information (which included my driver's license, registration, and insurance papers), a stolen vehicle raced past with two cop cars in pursuit. Our police officer immediately joined the chase, taking all my documentation with him. It was like a twist you'd see in a comedy. Last, I received the insurance claims check, and to my surprise, it was higher than the car's private sale or trade-in value.

I used to watch a show featuring homicide detective Joe Kenda. This man solved over 400 murder cases. Throughout the show, he would narrate some of the wisdom that he gained while solving the crimes. Many times, during his investigations, Joe Kenda uncovered critical pieces of evidence at just the right time. I often had the notion that maybe God was influencing the process to achieve justice. There always seemed to be far too many coincidences that ultimately helped crack the case. There's one statement from Joe Kenda that has stayed with me for all these years. He once said, "If it happens once, it's coincidence. If it happens twice, it's evidence."

As you read these pages, my goal is to motivate you to become an active participant in prayer. Maybe you question my truthfulness, accurate interpretation of the Bible's lessons, or you're offended by my doctrine, but I hope you can set aside those reservations. There is a way for you to seek the truth for yourself. You can conduct your own experiments and document the results. I invite you to try. God is real. I have experienced His engagement when I humble myself and ask. How you choose to respond to my invitation is entirely your decision. You can approach it with skepticism and mockery, or you can approach it with a sincere quest for answers. The choice is yours—scoff and mock or seek and knock.

"Come and hear, all ye that fear God, and I will declare what He hath done for my soul. I cried unto Him with my mouth, and He was extolled *(praised enthusiastically)* with my tongue. If I regard iniquity in my heart, the Lord will not hear me. But verily God hath heard me; He hath attended to the voice of my prayer. Blessed be God, who hath not turned away my prayer, nor His mercy from me!" (Psalm 66:16-20)

BUT WE WANT MORE!

I get it, you might look for more biblical support for this method of prayer. The good news is that there are plenty of examples. While the term 'fleece' draws attention to Gideon's prayer request, we can find a similar process in other instances throughout the Old Testament. I'll provide two more examples.

THE PHILISTINES AND THEIR MILK COWS

The Philistines successfully battled against the Israelites and subsequently gained possession of the Ark of the Covenant. This was a major victory for the Philistines, and the symbol of God's power was now behind enemy lines. The Philistines transported the Ark to their pagan temple and installed it next to their false idol, Dagon. God reacted.

"And the Philistines took the ark of God and brought it from Ebenezer unto Ashdod. When the Philistines took the ark of God, they brought it into the house of Dagon and set it by Dagon.

And when those of Ashdod arose early on the morrow, behold, Dagon had fallen upon his face to the earth before the ark of the Lord. And they took Dagon and set him in his place again.

And when they arose early on the morrow morning, behold, Dagon had fallen upon his face to the ground before the ark of the Lord; and the head of Dagon and both the palms of his hands were cut off upon the threshold; only the stump of Dagon was left to him. Therefore neither the priests of Dagon nor any who come into Dagon's house tread on the threshold of Dagon in Ashdod unto this day." (I Samuel 5:1-5)

The two nights passed, and two supernatural events occurred. Dagon's image had fallen prone before the Ark of the Covenant. The priests of Dagon became so frightened that they refused to enter the house of Dagon. They were right to be scared. A real God was displaying His genuine power. But God doesn't end there. God was not pleased.

"But the hand of the Lord was heavy upon those of Ashdod, and He destroyed them and smote them with hemorrhoids, even Ashdod and the borders thereof.
And when the men of Ashdod saw that it was so, they said, 'The ark of the God of Israel shall not abide with us, for his hand is sore upon us and upon Dagon our god.'
They sent therefore and gathered all the lords of the Philistines unto them and said, 'What shall we do with the ark of the God of Israel?' And they answered, 'Let the ark of the God of Israel be carried about unto Gath.'
And they carried the ark of the God of Israel about thither." (I Samuel 5:6-8)

The town of Ebenezer decided they don't want to keep the Ark because of the affliction it brought, so they opted to send it over to Gath. In a way, that course of action is humorous.

"And it was so that, after they had carried it about, the hand of the Lord was against the city with a very great destruction; and He smote the men of the city, both small and great, and they had hemorrhoids in their secret parts." (I Samuel 5:9)

Well, the plan to send the Ark to Gath didn't work out as intended. Gath faced significant destruction and even had the misfortune of developing hemorrhoids. It's almost like the saying goes, "With friends like the town of Ebenezer, who needs enemies?" But the Philistines made the same mistake once more. Gath sent the Ark to Ekron, and by that point, the word about the Ark and its disastrous effects was spreading.

A.S.K.

"Therefore they sent the ark of God to Ekron. And it came to pass, as the ark of God came to Ekron, that the Ekronites cried out, saying, 'They have brought about the ark of the God of Israel to us to slay us and our people.'

So they sent and gathered together all the lords of the Philistines and said, 'Send away the ark of the God of Israel, and let it go again to his own place, that it slay us not, and our people.' For there was a deadly destruction throughout all the city; the hand of God was very heavy there. And the men who died not were smitten with the hemorrhoids; and the cry of the city went up to heaven." (I Samuel 5:10-12)

This continued for seven months. I suppose the Philistines were slow learners. Eventually, they reached their breaking point and sought guidance from priests and diviners on a process for the safe return of the Ark to Israel. Israel's God and His Ark had caused them enough trouble. The priests and diviners devised a plan to address the situation.

"Now therefore make a new cart, and take two milk cows on which there hath come no yoke, and tie the cows to the cart and bring their calves home from them. And take the ark of the Lord and lay it upon the cart; and put the jewels of gold, which ye return to him for a trespass offering, in a coffer by the side thereof; and send it away, that it may go." (I Samuel 6:7-8)

The Philistines added a unique element to the plan. They incorporated a 'fleece' type experiment. While they seemed convinced that the true God of Israel was the source of their afflictions, they wanted to be certain.

"And see: If it goeth up by the way of his own coast to Bethshemesh, then he hath done us this great evil. But if not, then we shall know that it is not his hand that smote us; it was a chance that happened to us." (I Samuel 6:9)

The Philistines had a reputation for their wicked ways, regularly indulging in depravity and idolatry. Yet, they reached out to God to determine if He was truly involved in their circumstances. Inquiring minds wanted to know.

The first twist in their plan involved the use of milk cows, which were not typically used as draft animals. Milk cows aren't well-suited for pulling carts, and if you make them, their milk dries up. These two milk cows had never pulled a cart. They had never worn a yoke. The act of separating the cows from their calves caused them to experience stress. As you can see, the Philistines were trying to create a situation that would eliminate any notion of coincidence from their experiment. They were genuinely determined to find out if God was involved.

The second twist in their plan was to leave the stressed-out cows alone. No one guided or encouraged the cows to move. Have you ever seen milk cows wandering around a farmer's field? There is never a sense of urgency or direction. Cows simply meander around aimlessly. Expecting these two untrained milk cows, yoked to a cart and separated from their calves, to do anything other than stand around was a stretch.

With the cart and milk cows in place, the Philistines placed the Ark and offerings on the cart and then waited to witness the outcome. They had predetermined that if the cows were to return to Bethshemesh in Israel, it would serve as proof that the God of Israel was the force behind their afflictions. If the cows remained inactive or simply roamed about, they would conclude that their hardships were purely a matter of fate. You can probably guess what happened. God responded, even to this group of unbelieving idolaters.

"And the men did so; and took two milk cows and tied them to the cart, and shut up their calves at home. And they laid the ark of the Lord upon the cart, and the coffer with the mice of gold and the images of their hemorrhoids.
And the cows took the straight way to the way of Bethshemesh, and went along the highway, lowing as they went, and turned not aside to the right hand or to the left; and the lords of the Philistines

went after them unto the border of Bethshemesh." (I Samuel 6:10-12)

Two untrained milk cows, with no human prompting, made a beeline straight back to Israel. They didn't wander to either side of the road. I suspect many Philistines believed God from that day forward. They sought God in the best way they knew how, and God responded to their call. Even for these individuals who were pagan worshippers of Dagon, God provided an answer because they had asked.

GOING TO WAR WITHOUT WEAPONS

In the years following the return of the Ark to Israel, another important event occurs. As was often the case, the Philistines were causing many problems for Israel. They had subdued Israel, and subsequently removed all the blacksmiths from Israel to limit their ability to produce swords and spears for warfare. Whenever the Israelites needed to sharpen their plowshares, axes, or other farming tools, they had to travel to Philistine blacksmiths for help.

During this period, Saul was the King of Israel, and his son, Jonathan, had recently killed a garrison of the Philistines. Upon learning of this, the Philistine nation promptly declared war. As the Bible describes the Philistine army in the passage below, it's essential to note that Israel possessed no weapons, except for the two swords owned by King Saul and Jonathan.

"And the Philistines gathered themselves together to fight with Israel, thirty thousand chariots and six thousand horsemen, and people as the sand which is on the seashore in multitude. And they came up and pitched camp in Michmash, eastward from Bethaven.

When the men of Israel saw that they were in a strait (for the people were distressed), then the people hid themselves in caves and in thickets and in rocks and in high places and in pits. And some of the Hebrews went over the Jordan to the land of Gad and Gilead. As for Saul, he was yet in Gilgal, and all the people followed him trembling.

So it came to pass on the day of battle that there was neither sword nor spear found in the hand of any of the people who were with Saul and Jonathan, but with Saul and with Jonathan his son were they found." (I Samuel 13:5-7,22)

The Israelites found themselves in an unwinnable battle. Men were hiding while others were fleeing. However, Jonathan hatched a plan of action and implemented a 'fleece' like experiment.

"Now it came to pass upon a day that Jonathan, the son of Saul, said unto the young man who bore his armor, 'Come, and let us go over to the Philistines 'garrison that is on the other side.' But he told not his father.
And Jonathan said to the young man who bore his armor, 'Come, and let us go over unto the garrison of these uncircumcised. It may be that the Lord will work for us, for there is no restraint to the Lord to save by many or by few.'" (I Samuel 14:1,6)

As mentioned earlier, the Old Testament contains several noteworthy statements, and Jonathan's declaration is one worth remembering: "There is no restraint to the Lord, to save by many or by few." With these words in mind, Jonathan and his armorbearer set out, and Jonathan explained his 'fleece' experiment.

"Then said Jonathan, 'Behold, we will pass over unto these men, and we will disclose ourselves unto them. If they say thus unto us, 'Tarry until we come to you,' then we will stand still in our place and will not go up unto them. But if they say thus, 'Come up unto us,' then we will go up; for the Lord hath delivered them into our hand, and this shall be a sign unto us.'" (I Samuel 14:8-10)

If the Lord had chosen not to respond, there was a real risk that the Philistines would capture Jonathan and seek revenge for killing their garrison.

Jonathan also set a particular condition, a specific statement from the Philistines that he wished to hear, which would determine his course of action.

"And both of them revealed themselves unto the garrison of the Philistines; and the Philistines said, 'Behold, the Hebrews come forth out of the holes where they had hid themselves.' And the men of the garrison answered Jonathan and his armorbearer, and said, 'Come up to us, and we will show you a thing.'" (I Samuel 14:11)

The Philistines taunted Jonathan and then uttered the exact words Jonathan placed in his fleece: 'Come up to us'. The Philistine garrison wasn't afraid of two measly Israelites. But their real problem was the unseen God of Israel. It's like encountering a couple of cute, harmless bear cubs and failing to realize that the protective mama bear is lurking in the bushes. The Philistines were about to learn a lesson.

"And Jonathan said unto his armorbearer, 'Come up after me, for the Lord hath delivered them into the hand of Israel.'" (I Samuel 14:12)

Why did Jonathan have such confidence? His life was at stake. It's a question worth pondering. If he was wrong, he was going to suffer torture and most likely die. Yet, there is no sign of doubt in his actions. This was the essence of the faith in God brought forth through a 'prayer fleece'. Jonathan's faith in God allowed him to act with confidence in the spoken words of a group of Philistines he had no control over, having the faith to trust that God responded to his specific prayer.

"And Jonathan climbed up upon his hands and upon his feet, and his armorbearer after him. And they fell before Jonathan, and his armorbearer slew after him. And that first slaughter which Jonathan and his armorbearer made was about twenty men within, as it were, a half acre of land which a yoke of oxen might plow. And there was trembling in the host, in the field, and among all the people. The garrison and the despoilers also trembled, and the earth quaked; so it was a very great trembling. And the watchmen of Saul in Gibeah of Benjamin looked; and behold, the multitude melted away, and they went on beating down one another. (I Samuel 14:13-16)

The story of the Ark's seven-month holiday in Philistine territory set the stage for the victory, because the Philistines had already experienced the power of God. As word of Jonathan's victory over twenty men circulated, a chain reaction ensued. Fear gripped the Philistines, and they quickly retreated. In the withdrawal's chaos, panic set in, and they violently turned on each other.

The faith of Jonathan, who employed the method of seeking God's direction through a fleece experiment, started a series of events that proved to be unstoppable.

DIRECTIONS NEEDED

God has provided a written blueprint for how we should lead our lives, yet we encounter specific choices that are unique to each of us. These decisions can encompass an array of choices, including who to date, who to marry, which job to accept, which house to buy, which church to attend, which town to live in, which pet to adopt, which medical treatment to pursue, how to offer counsel to a friend, how to navigate the challenges of raising a child in the age of social media and AI, and that's just a tiny fraction of life's choices.

What decisions would you face if society were to collapse, or war arrived on your doorstep, or food became scarce? Americans are presently navigating rather shallow waters, but how are you going to navigate deep and dangerous waters? How will you know whether to turn to the right or the left, metaphorically speaking?

My advice is to become an active participant in seeking God, acknowledge Him, and conduct your own experiments with 'prayer fleeces'. In addition, read your Bible, use its examples, and gain the confidence to trust God to direct your path.

A.S.K.

IT CAN WORK FOR YOU TOO

I've shared these prayer concepts with people over many years. Occasionally, a small few have taken it upon themselves to experiment and later report their findings. The following are two examples. Remember Joe Kenda's words, "If it happens once, it's coincidence. If it happens twice, it's evidence."

The first story involved my family. I've taught in church frequently, and my children found themselves stuck in the audience. The great thing about this situation is that I can direct some of the lesson toward them without being obvious. If you are a parent, you know it's hard to sit a kid down and have them listen to instruction. So, I used these opportunities to offer indirect instruction through Bible lessons.

My son was no stranger to my fleece experiment concept; he had heard me talk about it many times. When he was in high school, he grappled with a decision he couldn't quite make. I had taught him that, just like Jonathan, the fleece must be something specific and beyond your control. You can't put your thumb on the scales, so to speak. Identifying an appropriate 'fleece' can often take a great deal of contemplation.

Being a clever young man, he came up with an idea. I don't recommend this fleece for anyone because of its obvious implications, but he was still young and unafraid. His chosen fleece was to trip and fall during his day. He prayed that if he did trip and fall, it would be a sign to guide his course of action. Otherwise, he would proceed with the alternative decision. As you know, tripping and falling are out of your control. You don't actively plan to trip or fall; it just happens unexpectedly.

My son offered this prayer one morning, headed off to school, got caught up in the day's activities, and soon forgot about his request. But God didn't forget.

Midway through the afternoon, while descending the school stairs, my son tripped and fell three steps down onto the staircase's intermediate landing. The good news was that God spared him embarrassment because there weren't many witnesses. So, was this just a coincidence, or is it evidence?

As a bonus, my son felt a genuine thrill when God engaged with him and answered his prayer. I felt a similar exhilaration when the accident totaled my car. It's an amazing moment when you recognize there's direct proof that God heard your prayer.

I like to imagine a scene in heaven where God gathered His angels and said, "Attention, I need someone to trip this young man today. Ensure he's not hurt, and spare him too much embarrassment, but make it memorable enough that he remembers his prayer." And then the host of angels eagerly volunteered, saying, "I'll do it, pick me!"

The second story came from a close family friend. She's a grown woman who had heard my son's story. Against my warning, she found the idea of tripping and falling to seek guidance appealing. She was facing a weighty decision and had been praying and fasting, yet she remained indecisive. God wasn't discernibly responding.

In her prayer for guidance via a trip and fall 'fleece', she added more specifics to the request. She prayed for an injury of some sort. Again, it's not the approach I would recommend, but she didn't consult me. Within a few days, she tripped and fell, hitting her head hard enough to give her a migraine headache. She contemplated going to the hospital (it was that bad) but attended a major college football game instead (who can blame her). At the late fall pregame tailgate, she stood too close to a space heater, and her coat caught fire.

Later, sitting in the football stadium with a throbbing headache and burned coat, she realized this was what she had prayed for. She had her answer and knew what course of action to take.

The prayer fleece requires faith. And it works. If you acknowledge God, ask for His direction, then He will direct your path.

BACK TO MY BIG PRAYER

At the conclusion of Chapter 3, I ended with a cliffhanger. While praying for God to expose and uproot the corruption in our government and culture, I knew such a request would take a significant amount of time to materialize. Therefore, I wanted a preview to determine if God would answer my prayer. I spent several days trying to think of a suitable fleece experiment when I remembered the Netflix documentary "Making a Murderer", the events of which took place around 2007. While people have speculated that the documentary skewed the facts to present the two men as innocent, I was reflecting on their struggle.

A.S.K.

So, I thought to myself, "I should ask God to intervene on their behalf, maybe get them out of jail, assuming they were innocent, of course." But then I think to myself, "That's probably too big of a fleece. After all, they have been in jail since 2007, and it has been nine years, and the wheels of justice move slowly, so it's probably not the right fleece experiment to request." I abandoned the idea, never uttering the prayer.

Instead, I spent the next three days contemplating what kind of fleece experiment to request, but I couldn't come up with anything that seemed substantial. Then, on August 12th, 2016, I open the news and read the headline, "Conviction Against Brendan Dassey of 'Making a Murderer' Is Overturned."

It took only three days for a fleece experiment that I never formally requested, and instead abandoned because of lack of faith, to unfold in the news. I am still dumbfounded by this. How do you explain the timing of these unrelated events? It can't possibly be a coincidence. The statistical improbability of my abandoned prayer and the overturning of a conviction occurring within just 72 hours is too significant to ignore. I know how it happens because God is real, but it's still hard to wrap my mind around. Prayer matters and prayer works. God hears our prayers if we abandon our sinful ways and follow Jesus.

To be fair, I haven't kept up with the ongoing legal developments related to 'Making a Murderer'. Since then, someone requested an appeal, leaving both men imprisoned. Regardless, this series of events has continued to maintain my attention.

"Behold, I am the Lord, the God of all flesh. Is there any thing too hard for Me?" (Jeremiah 32:27)

The outcomes of my fleece experiments have increased my faith. They have reinforced the truth that God is real, and nothing is too difficult for him. I'm not putting God to the test; I'm placing my trust in Him. My attitude in these matters is not driven by a need for proof, but a genuine inquiry for guidance in navigating challenging times and making hard decisions. I don't need God to prove Himself; I already have faith in Him and His Word. Nothing will change that. The Bible encourages us to experience God for ourselves. It's like telling a friend about a delicious dish, but describing the meal is never enough. You always want your friends to taste it themselves so they can savor the wonderful flavor. So, don't just take my word for it; taste and see that the Lord is good.

"O taste and see that the Lord is good: blessed is the man that trusteth in him." (Psalm 34:8)

A.S.K.

5

Big Prayers

5

Big Prayers

Nothing is impossible for God. The Bible states it repeatedly. As I reflected on these declarations, a thought crossed my mind: "Perhaps the issue lies within me—maybe my faith is lacking."

I'm human, grappling with all the same frailties and failings as you. My doubts and my sin are ever present. No matter how hard I try, my heart still beats with an inclination towards wickedness. My tongue can carve up friend and foe alike. The cares of this life too often occupy both my time and my thoughts. I spend too much time thinking about myself rather than contemplating God and meditating on His Word. My only hope is Jesus Christ and His promises. God's Word leads me down narrow and hidden paths I would never discover on my own, and my life has benefited from adhering to His commandments.

Over the years, my contemplations led me to a decision: to pray for something big. After all, I had been learning to pray for 15+ years. Little by little, my faith grew because I read the Bible. Within its pages, I encountered new thoughts and ideas, and then tried to experiment by putting these Biblical concepts into practice. The more things happened, the more my faith grew.

In my life, one fleece after another received answers. The subsequent paths I followed in response to these answers led to great benefit. The same held true for my wife; her prayer fleeces received answers, and we often shared our experiences, occasionally tackling problems together through prayer. My children and friends have put their own prayer fleeces into practice, and God kept responding, again and again.

A.S.K.

I kept pushing the boundaries, yet I found no barriers. Maybe there are no barriers. I decided to go BIG.

"And Jesus, looking upon them, said, 'With men it is impossible, but not with God; for with God all things are possible.'" (Mark 10:27)

The question I wrestled with was whether I genuinely believed Jesus' statement. Could I offer a big prayer, while wholeheartedly believing that God would answer? The act of praying the big prayer is the simple part. The real challenge was looking within myself and truly inspecting my level of faith.

With God, all things are possible. I'm reminded of the story of Nebuchadnezzar, the King of Babylon, who cast three men into a furnace so scorching hot that it consumed the guards tasked with tossing the Israelites into the fire. Yet, these three Israelites walked out unharmed.

"Jesus said unto him, 'If thou canst believe, all things are possible to him that believeth.' And straightway the father of the child cried out and said with tears, 'Lord, I believe; help Thou mine unbelief!'" (Mark 9:23-24)

Jesus stated, "If you can believe." And that's the crux of the entire effort. Uttering prayers is easy, but can you believe? Can you honestly look at yourself in the mirror, and without doubt, believe that God will hear and answer your prayer?

In this story, the man's response to Jesus is perfect. He exclaims, "Lord, I believe; help my unbelief." I would say this is true of me as well. I believe, yet unbelief still lingers. This prayer is a good starting point for anyone. If you lack faith, then begin by asking God to increase your faith.

A GRAND EXPERIMENT #1

Many people frequently mention the following quote from Jesus.

> "Jesus answered and said unto them, 'Verily I say unto you, if ye have faith and doubt not, ye shall not only do this which is done to the fig tree, but also if ye shall say unto this mountain, 'Be thou removed and be thou cast into the sea,' it shall be done. And all things whatsoever ye shall ask in prayer, believing, ye shall receive.'" (Matthew 21:21-22)

Keep in mind that this is only one statement about prayer. To gain a comprehensive understanding of what God teaches about prayer, you need to examine the entire scope of the Bible. Relying solely on these two verses as your guide to prayer would be like finding a twig and claiming you know all about every tree in the forest.

However, these two verses provide valuable knowledge. First, you must possess faith without doubt. This is such a demanding requirement, a narrow gate, that few will pass through. Instead of focusing on moving a physical mountain, focus on the unseen mountain of your own doubt and your own lack of faith. This is the first mountain that must move.

> "Enter ye in at the strait gate, for wide is the gate and broad is the way that leadeth to destruction, and many there be who go in thereat. Because strait is the gate, and narrow is the way which leadeth unto life, and few there be that find it." (Matthew 7:13-14)

Jesus asserted that prayer has the power to move mountains. Jesus verbally cursed a fig tree and the next day it was dead. I believe that through prayer, a mountain can move. Yet, we cannot forget the other critical facet of prayer—discerning God's will. Ask yourself these questions—Is it God's will for Christians to be remodeling the Earth at will? What would be the purpose?

While I could pray for God to move a physical mountain and use these verses as my inspiration, I need to answer the question of 'why'. Why should

A.S.K.

God move a mountain? What is my reasoning for making such a request? Personally, I cannot think of a single valid argument that would get God's serious consideration.

Satan attempted to use Biblical quotes to tempt Jesus in the wilderness, but his intentions were not sincere. He was trying to manipulate God into an action. He was being deceitful. Satan's request was based on mockery and cynicism.

If you were to ask God to move a mountain merely out of curiosity or a desire to test God, then God could easily reply, "Who are you to contend with God? Observe the world around you; the evidence of My existence is manifest in the intricate details of creation. I have already proven Myself. Examine the leaf on a tree, or your own anatomy, or the splendor of the animal kingdom. Proof is everywhere. If you cannot grasp this, then moving a mountain or witnessing a resurrection from the dead won't penetrate your hardened heart."

The Bible describes a narrow path of faith. A path often has two opposing sides. In this example, on one side of the path lies the temptation to manipulate God into action by perverting His words. These attempts will encounter resistance. You cannot mock God.

But there is an opposite side of the narrow path. On the other side lies the danger of inaction. Neglecting to put into practice the teachings of Jesus is problematic. It's like receiving the proverbial talent and then burying it in the sand because of fear or apathy. I would submit that inaction is as bad as tempting God.

Hence, the motivation and reasoning behind your prayer request is important. If you cannot convince yourself that your prayer is free from envy, lust, greed, or some other selfish desire, it is probably best to reconsider your request.

Meanwhile, strive to believe that God has no limits.

The intersection of these concepts led me to think that I should pray bigger. As I mentioned earlier, I wondered if the colossal problems of the world remained unsolved because many Christians don't pray. Or perhaps they primarily pray for their personal needs. If my observations are accurate, then who is praying for the issues that impact billions of lives?

In 2016, I considered one such problem, a challenge so vast that it continues to baffle the brightest minds. Many world leaders have failed to find a workable solution. We're into the third generation and the problem persists without an end in sight. It's a stalemate. There is no hope. There is only a simmering confrontation.

The problem is North Korea.

I embarked on my ambitious experiment, focused on praying for North Korea. To ensure some witnesses in case of success, I confided in a select few. My plan involved dedicating 2017 to prayer and fasting, focused only on North Korea. Each week, on a designated day—usually Tuesdays—I would fast. This entailed having my last meal on Monday, skipping all meals on Tuesday, and resuming my regular eating schedule on Wednesday morning. I figured that an unsolvable problem was one of those prayers that needed fasting.

In addition, I spent several weeks thinking about the contents of the specific prayer and working it over in my mind. Drawing from my earlier analogy, I was like a lawyer preparing opening statements for a judge. Once I formed the prayer with my reasonings, I offered a request that resembled the following.

"Lord, I believe you can do anything, just like You said. There is no restraint with the LORD to help with many or few. The Korean war has never ended. This is a 70+ year old problem. There are 25+ million North Koreans living in a communist police state with no access to the truth of Jesus Christ and the gospel. An entire generation of North Koreans need to hear the gospel. They live in abject poverty. They live in constant fear of the government. The stories that leak out show that the communist party government preys upon the people and even forcefully takes wives and young girls for their own pleasure and rapes them. There is no justice. No recourse. They've had famines where people were eating the bark off the trees to survive. Bibles are illegal. In their isolation, I suspect that most do not know the hope that Jesus offers. God, you know all this. You are a witness to the oppression and the plight of the people of North Korea. They are prisoners to a power-hungry ruler, his generals, and the communist system. Jesus said that the fields were ripe with harvest, and perhaps there is no greater gospel harvest field in the world today than North Korea. However, this harvest cannot happen unless the borders are open and there is religious freedom available. North Korea's communist wall must fall. The people must be free to hear the gospel. There are 25+ million reasons this should happen. This is a problem that no man can solve. The enormity of the problem is beyond human capability. The only resolution is with You, GOD, and You alone. Only You can intervene and make a change. This is easily within Your power. You said that You are not willing that any should perish, but that

A.S.K.

all would come to You in repentance for salvation. Please open North Korea to the gospel and fix this festering problem. Amen."

That was the essence of the prayer. I would incorporate variations over time as I thought of additional scriptures that I could apply to the reasoning. Immediately, something happened. Early in 2017, North Korea dominated the daily headlines. This was not a passing story that quickly faded; it lingered throughout the entire year and into 2018. Was this a coincidence?

By 2018, a historic and unprecedented event occurred when the American President, Donald Trump, visited the Demilitarized Zone (DMZ) and held a meeting with the leader of North Korea. Something different was developing in front of the entire world. I couldn't help but wonder if God was moving a mountain.

Since that pivotal moment in 2018, there has been a noticeable reduction in the news emanating from North Korea. Does that mean my prayer failed? Does that mean that God isn't working? Honestly, I do not know. Neither do you. No one has access to any data points. In addition, the answer to this prayer will be a process over time, not a specific event. Only the rearview mirror of history will expose the truth.

But that's perfectly okay. My situational awareness is not important. North Korea, often referred to as the 'hermit kingdom', has successfully hidden itself from the world for decades. Nobody really knows what's happening inside the country. The government of North Korea has extensively brainwashed the people. If God is liberating them, He might need to spend time to deprogram the communist culture. In the grand scheme of things, even if it takes 10 or 20 years, it's a relatively insignificant span of time. Meanwhile, my prayer fills me with hope. I look forward to the afterlife, where I will gain insight into the specific details of what God was doing with North Korea during this era and whether my pleading held any significance.

This is certain: God heard my prayer, and He saw my fasting. He knows that I'm not attempting to manipulate Him with this request. I have no selfish desires intertwined with this prayer and I have nothing personal to gain from this. God loves North Koreans. I know God can easily change North Korea. So, I pray He will.

If you are thinking about becoming a missionary, it might be beneficial to learn the Korean language. I'll just throw that out there for someone.

The journey of praying bigger has increased my faith. Lately, I've pondered whether our lack of faith might cause God to withhold His power. The Bible passage below is interesting. It shows unbelieving people who affected Jesus' ministry.

"And when He had come into His own country, He taught them in their synagogue, insomuch that they were astonished and said, 'From whence hath this man this wisdom and these mighty works? Is not this the carpenter's son? Is not his mother called Mary and his brethren James and Joseph, and Simon and Judas? And his sisters, are they not all with us? From whence then hath this man all these things?' And they were offended at Him. But Jesus said unto them, 'A prophet is not without honor, save in his own country and in his own house.'

And He did not many mighty works there, because of their unbelief." (Matthew 13:54-58)

The last statement in the passage above is very insightful. Jesus didn't perform many mighty works because the people didn't believe. God's power was not low on batteries. God chose not to work because nobody believed.

A GRAND EXPERIMENT #2

Fasting once a week for an entire year is a demanding commitment, and if you ever try it, you'll quickly discover just how challenging it can be. It often felt like there were three Tuesdays in a week. When I would struggle with hunger, I would try to motivate myself by saying to my wife, "I am so hungry and miserable, but you know who else is hungry and miserable right now? The North Koreans". While the issues in North Korea were simmering in the background, I tried another prayer in 2019 to see if there were similar results to what transpired during 2017.

My next big prayer was for a spiritual revival in America, focusing on the minority communities trapped in a never-ending doom-loop of poverty in the major cities.

A.S.K.

Having lived in the suburbs of urban Detroit for 19 years, I witnessed firsthand the decay of the city. Politicians in Detroit and the State of Michigan have proposed many solutions to address the issues of poverty, crime, low graduation rates, and shockingly, the 47% illiteracy rate. Yes, 47% illiteracy! Detroit is just one example, as this challenge plagues cities across the nation. It's a vicious downward spiral. I could devote my entire life trying to make a difference for the residents of Detroit, but the problem is too big, and I'm too small. In addition, I don't have even an inkling of an idea of where to start. And neither does anyone else. But I know One who does. God knows how to turn the tables.

So, I applied the same process I had used when praying for the North Koreans. I took time to reflect on my request and then offered a prayer that went something like this:

"LORD, I've been here on earth for nearly 50 years. The problems in our cities only grows worse. There are programs after programs, and untold amounts of government money being spent, but none of it's having an impact. Things continue to spiral down, and people are suffering. The only answer is Jesus. There are no other answers. There are no solutions, there are no programs, and money isn't the answer. Something must change on the inside. Your Spirit must work on a mass scale. I believe that You are willing to do this if we ask because of Your ministry on earth. The Bible says that when You looked out on the masses of people, You had compassion on them because they were like sheep without a shepherd. You would spend long hours to the point of exhaustion healing people, counseling people, and teaching people. Apart from Your private prayer time, You were always reaching out with love and compassion. You spent Your time with the poor, the uneducated, the despondent, the sick, and the sinner. People in my country are in these same situations. I'm asking that You pour out Your Spirit on my countrymen and stir their hearts and minds to You. I'm asking that You reach into the hopeless situations and use these forgotten people to rise and turn our nation back to God. You said in the Bible that God uses the base and foolish things of the world to confound the wise. There is no more unlikely place than the poor, illiterate, and despondent inner cities for Your light to shine. No one is looking for answers to come from the poor, which makes for a perfect plan. Only You can take credit for a spiritual renaissance. In years to come, when these former wastelands of cities transform into crime-free and prosperous communities with healthy and happy people, my prayer is that the wise, the highly educated, the media, and the politicians ask, 'How did this happen?'. And the people reply, 'It is because of Jesus, and our decision to follow Him and His commandments, and what you see results from that decision.' The elites cannot condemn or silence these people without appearing to be racist. In a way, the elites will become caught in a trap they have created. I want to see a day when all can witness Your transformative power, and the formerly hopeless and forgotten people of our nation openly declare Jesus as the reason for this transformation. That Your light would shine bright. You have a parable where a man made a great supper and invited many—And sent his servant at supper time to say to them, 'Come; for all things are now ready.' And they all, with one consent, made excuses. The first said unto him, 'I have bought a piece of ground, and I must need see it: I pray thee have me excused.' And another said, 'I have bought five yoke of oxen, and I go to prove them: I pray thee have me excused.' And another said, 'I have married a wife, and therefore I cannot come.' So that servant came and shewed his lord these things. Then the master of the house being angry said to his servant, 'Go out quickly into the streets and lanes of the city, and bring in hither the poor, and the maimed, and the halt, and the blind.' And the servant said, 'Lord, it is done, as thou have commanded, and yet there is room.' And the lord said unto the servant, 'Go out into the highways and hedges, and compel them to come in, that my house may be filled.' I'm asking for Your house to be filled with the poor and forgotten people of my nation. Amen."

As for my 2019 prayer, the result remains to be determined. A change of this magnitude takes time. However, in 2020, there was a significant worldwide focus on the death of a black man in police custody and the subsequent rise of many political organizations. The streets filled with protests and cities burned.

Was this all a coincidence? I'm not suggesting that the events of the summer of 2020 were positive, nor do I endorse the wicked philosophies and Marxist policies that emerged during that time. But the timing of these events certainly makes me wonder. When God works, it never seems to be in a straight line. King Solomon referenced this in his writings.

"Consider the work of God; for who can make straight that which He hath made crooked?" (Ecclesiastes 7:13)

Notice that this verse seems backwards. We often expect God to make things straight, yet the verse talks about God making things crooked. Sometimes, it appears God might be at work, but from our daily perspective, things appear to be in disarray. Perhaps God has a plan unfolding, and with time, the brilliance of that plan will become clear.

So, those are two of my ambitious prayer experiments I'm willing to share. The results remain inconclusive, but it's striking how closely both prayers align with major news events that continue to shape the world.

I realize correlation does not equal causation. My goal is not to elevate myself. My goal is to get you to think. We could argue about whether the evidence presented is compelling, or if I have simple confirmation bias, but that is not the point. My goal is to get you to experiment with prayer on your own. Do your own research and decide.

I have another experiment that I'm forming. This will be another 'big prayer' attempt, and I'm eager to see if the previous patterns emerge once again.

Does any of this convince you to try praying big? I hope so. There are countless major issues in the world that could benefit from prayer. Recently, I came across a Christian group organizing a conference to tackle a thorny topic. Maybe this is good, but I think Christian conferences will not change the world. I think private prayers from righteous individuals with unwavering faith in a real God will change the world.

If you are thinking about trying this out, consider selecting a big problem that bothers you. It could be any of the pressing issues: poverty, crime, sex trafficking, slavery, corruption of sexual mores, corruption in government, illicit drugs, drunkenness, pharmaceuticals, depraved music lyrics, sexism, racism, inequality, wars, disease, dirty water, the drug cartels - you get my point.

I encourage you to pray big.

"'For the oppression of the poor, for the sighing of the needy, now will I arise,' saith the Lord; 'I will set him in safety from him that puffeth at him.'" (Psalm 12:5)

A.S.K.

6

Pray for One Another

A.S.K.

6

Pray for One Another

When I was much younger, there was a fellow church member who repeatedly asked, "How can I pray for you?". I often wondered if this was a sincere question or an attempt to gather interesting gossip.

Around the same time, there was a man who would come to me and say, "I'm praying that God will make you a millionaire!" I would smile and reply, "Thank you, that is very kind." Then I'd turn to my wife and humorously ask her if it would be appropriate to ask him to change millionaire to multimillionaire. After all, if he's praying, why stop at a million? But looking back, with age and wisdom, I should have asked for just one letter to change: turning the M into a B. Or maybe a Z.

Listen, while I appreciate someone praying for my financial well-being, I've learned that there are more substantial things in life that hold far greater value than just health and wealth. The Bible provides a list of life's valuable elements that we can use as prayer topics when praying for one another. The Apostle Paul often requested prayer or mentioned that he was praying specific prayers for others. I've listed several of these verses below, followed by a summarized list of twelve prayer topics.

This is not an exhaustive list. It focuses your attention on the concept of praying for spiritual ideals. I think that if we focus on praying for spiritual health, then the answers will manifest themselves in both the spiritual and the physical. Perhaps there is a truth we have missed. Instead of focusing most of our prayers on the physical matters of our existence, if we pray for spiritual blessings, then the physical blessings will naturally follow. According to Jesus, if we prioritize seeking the kingdom of God and His righteousness, He will take care of our physical needs (Matthew 6:33).

"For God is my witness, whom I serve with my spirit in the Gospel of His Son, that without ceasing I make mention of you always in my prayers," (Romans 1:9)

"Finally, brethren, pray for us, that the Word of the Lord may have free course and be glorified, even as it is with you, and that we may be delivered from unreasonable and wicked men; for not all men have faith." (II Thessalonians 3:1-2)

"Therefore also we pray always for you, that our God would count you worthy of this calling, and fulfill all the good pleasure of His goodness and the work of faith with power, that the name of our Lord Jesus Christ may be glorified in you, and ye in Him, according to the grace of our God and the Lord Jesus Christ." (II Thessalonians 1:11-12)

"…besides praying also for us that God would open unto us a door of utterance to speak the mystery of Christ, for which I am also in bonds," (Colossians 4:3)

"For this cause we also, since the day we heard it, do not cease to pray for you and to desire that ye might be filled with the knowledge of His will in all wisdom and spiritual understanding; that ye might walk worthy of the Lord, in all pleasing Him, being fruitful in every good work, and increasing in the knowledge of God; strengthened with all might according to His glorious power, unto all patience and longsuffering with joyfulness; giving thanks unto the Father," (Colossians 1:9-12)

"And this I pray, that your love may abound yet more and more in knowledge and in all judgment," (Philippians 1:9)

A.S.K.

"...cease not to give thanks for you, making mention of you in my prayers. I pray that the God of our Lord Jesus Christ, the Father of glory, may give unto you the spirit of wisdom and revelation in the knowledge of Him, the eyes of your understanding being enlightened, that ye may know what is the hope of His calling, and what are the riches of the glory of His inheritance in the saints, and what is the exceeding greatness of His power toward us who believe, according to the working of His mighty power," (Ephesians 1:16-19)

Paul's prayers didn't focus on the physical health of the church members, which is a common theme on many modern prayer lists. Paul's primary concern lay in the spiritual health of the congregation. He prayed for their wisdom, knowledge, understanding, and their hope in God. He prayed they would come to know the greatness of the Lord and of His great power.

When Paul requested prayer from others, he didn't seek healing for his own physical ailment (although he had one). Instead, look at Paul's request.

"...praying always with all prayer and supplication in the Spirit, and watching thereunto with all perseverance and supplication for all saints. And pray for me, that utterance may be given unto me, that I may open my mouth boldly to make known the mystery of the Gospel," (Ephesians 6:18-19)

Paul's request focused on the ability to communicate the gospel effectively. Apparently, he found this need more important than his lingering health problem. It's a thought-provoking perspective that encourages us to reevaluate how we pray for one another.

I'm not disregarding the need for physical healing because ailments can bring about substantial challenges and consume all your focus, as well as the focus of those around you. I understand that it's difficult to pray when your back is screaming in agony and sleep is fleeting. If you need physical healing, then think about why the Judge should grant your request. Is your request rooted in your own lusts? Or perhaps a better question to consider is: What will you do differently if you were in better health? Would you genuinely use your newfound health to seek God's kingdom and His righteousness, or would you simply pursue earthly pleasure and indulgence? I believe these questions need proper answers before forming your healing prayer.

I have noticed a few things about human nature. People often criticize the aspects they don't like about others. I'm an expert critic, and I suspect you are as well. Criticism is prevalent in all aspects of life, including church. Human nature doesn't magically disappear because you passed through the front door of a church. Critical and complaining attitudes are challenging to overcome. None of us are exempt from these behaviors.

However, there might be a way to break the cycle. I wonder: What would happen if we attempted to train ourselves to pray for the spiritual health of one another, as the Bible encourages? Perhaps it would become increasingly difficult to be critical of others. If you are earnestly praying for someone to gain wisdom and understanding, you might find it harder to call them a stupid moron. If they are a moron, perhaps your prayer request will be successful, and they will become less idiotic. Or maybe, just maybe, your attitude towards that person might lighten up a little and you'll be less critical. The only way to know for sure is to try praying for one another.

Imagine the impact if God answered our prayers for spiritual health. What if God genuinely fostered spiritual growth, and when we asked for more, He provided without an upper limit? Imagine if people could change and grow spiritually, rather than always being destined to remain as they are. What if old dogs learned new tricks?

THE PRAYER LIST I'D LIKE TO SEE AT CHURCH

ONE: "That the word of the Lord may have free course."

This indeed is a foundational prayer. The Bible serves as the solid rock upon which we can build our lives. Therefore, praying that the Word of the Lord would work freely in our hearts and minds and culture with no hinderance, or restraint would truly change us for the better.

A.S.K.

In the parable of the sower and the seed, the seed is the Word of God. If the Word of God has a free course, it would find fertile ground more frequently.

Think about this for a moment. If the word of the Lord were to have free course in the world, what would change?

The key word here is free, as in freedom. Consider the governments of the world today. Most do not allow religious freedom. If this one prayer were to be answered, then several totalitarian governments in the world would transform. Cultures everywhere would be impacted for the better.

As a Christian in America, you could pray for the country. But why? You might conclude that you want to protect the freedoms enshrined in the Constitution and the Bill of Rights. But why do you want these freedoms to be protected? You know the answer. We need these freedoms so that the word of the Lord may have free course. This prayer IS a prayer for America. No other form of human government allows for such a free course for the word of the Lord. None.

TWO: "Delivered from unreasonable and wicked men."

This is a prayer for deliverance. We live in a time of unreasonable and wicked men. It's clear that much of what's happening lacks any common sense. Solutions exist, but people ignore the obvious resolution. The ability to engage in reasonable discussion is nearly impossible. Given the number of unreasonable people in the world with harmful intentions, it's a wise prayer to ask for deliverance from their wicked schemes. Notice we aren't asking for their destruction or for God to take vengeance. Rather, we seek to be delivered from their wicked devices.

Proverbs touches on a relevant idea that addresses God's will for the unreasonable and wicked men: "Whoso diggeth a pit shall fall therein, and he that rolleth a stone, it will return upon him" (Proverbs 26:27). This principle underscores the consequences that come to those who plot harm.

When I was a child, I enjoyed playing the board game called Life. One pitfall of the game was a spot labeled 'SUED for $100,000'. I always thought legal problems would be a terrible real-life dilemma, and I hoped it would never happen to me. As the number of unreasonable and wicked men multiply, our prayer for each other should include this request for deliverance. We will never rid ourselves of the unreasonable, but we can pray for deliverance from their wicked schemes.

THREE: "That our God would count you worthy of this calling, fulfill all the good pleasure of his goodness, and the work of faith with power."

God's grace saved us from our sins. Now, He has given us some work to do. We have a calling and a purpose that drives our lives. Faith drives the work, and the combination of faith with God's power serves as a significant catalyst for good.

FOUR: "...the name of our Lord Jesus Christ may be glorified in you, and ye in him, walk worthy of the Lord."

This prayer is a request that each of us can rise to the challenge of being called 'Christian'. This is a vital concept because it's often how we act that leaves a lasting impression. Our behavior and actions are significant. It's not uncommon to encounter individuals who identify as Christian, but their actions can be puzzling or contradictory. None of us can claim to be without flaws, so we all need prayers that request God's help with our behavior. Our lifestyles should rise to the level that is worthy of representing our Lord.

The goal is to be distinctly different in our actions, which ultimately brings glory to the name of our Lord Jesus Christ. Our way of living should attract people to Christ, not repel them.

FIVE: "That God would open unto us a door of utterance, to speak the mystery of Christ."

Have you ever experienced that post-conversation feeling where you replay in your mind all the things you should have said? If you are like me, it's sometimes difficult to communicate properly. This can happen in a variety of situations, but when someone is open to discussing spiritual matters, we want the ability to articulate the gospel clearly.

Explaining spiritual concepts in a way that is understandable can be quite challenging, especially when the other person lacks basic knowledge of the Bible. If you're not careful, you might speak in a way that goes over their heads, using terms like 'propitiation' and 'sanctification' that they've never encountered in a meaningful context. We should regularly request that God would grant us the ability to communicate the gospel effectively.

SIX: "Being fruitful in every good work,"

It's good to work, but if there are no results, then what is the point? One year, I toiled for months over a vegetable garden, and in the end, all I reaped was a single, tiny pepper. It was the most expensive and labor-intensive pepper ever grown. My daughter and I conducted a little two-minute ceremony to celebrate the pepper, and then we ate it. It tasted terrible. I no longer have a garden.

We don't want our spiritual efforts to be as unrewarding as my gardening—toilsome and unfruitful. To maintain motivation in our spiritual work, it's crucial to see some level of results. Therefore, this is a motivating prayer for one another. When answered, it can help us persevere and stay committed to our spiritual journey, despite the challenges we may face.

SEVEN: "Strengthened with all might."

Strength is important. I resumed weightlifting in my 40s, and it's made certain aspects of life much easier because everything seems lighter. I could carry all the grocery bags into the kitchen on a single trip if I chose to. Yes, I'm really that strong.

This concept holds true for your spiritual strength. When we possess spiritual strength, the obstacles and opposition we encounter appear less intimidating. The tasks ahead will seem less burdensome, and we will have a better ability to confront life's challenges. Spiritual strength can effectively prepare your mind to handle a wide range of difficult situations.

But hidden in the spiritual focus of the prayer is a physical aspect. You could pray for a physical ailment, but maybe a better prayer is for strength, both physically and spiritually, for serving Him more fully.

EIGHT: "Strengthened with all patience and long-suffering with joyfulness."

Life can get hard. It will wear you down and drain your motivation. Life doesn't have the best track record for consistency. Problems don't come one at a time; often, they come in multiples, with new ones continually arising. It can feel overwhelming. What we truly need is to be strengthened with patience and then add long-suffering. And on top of that, add joy.

We should pray for the ability to endure long-term challenges and do so with a joyful spirit. This is quite a combination - patience, long-suffering, and joy.

Typically, when someone tests your patience, it's easy to feel irritated. But if God grants us the strength to develop patience and long-suffering while maintaining a cheerful disposition, we will undoubtedly stand out in the crowd. People will notice because the combination of these characteristics is rare.

And once you get noticed, what would happen if the previously mentioned prayers also got answered? If the door of utterance opens so that you can freely speak the mysteries of Christ, and if you become fruitful unto every good work and receive strength with all might, then the results would be truly amazing.

NINE: "Giving thanks unto the Father."

We should strive to make this a consistent practice. God is the source of our salvation, and the very source of our existence. We should always remember our position in relation to Him and His role in our lives. Regardless of the circumstances we face, there is always something to be grateful for. By concentrating on gratitude rather than dwelling on the negatives, you'll notice a positive shift in your perspective on life.

A.S.K.

TEN: "That love may abound."

Love is a fragile thing; it can easily grow cold. Jesus warned, "And because iniquity shall abound, the love of many shall wax cold" (Matthew 24:12).

We seem to have reached a cultural stage where the abundance of iniquity is extinguishing love. It's disheartening to see the many examples of people passing by others in need, much like the characters in the parable of the Good Samaritan. It seems people decline to engage because our experiences have taught us to perceive a situation as a potential threat first, instead of seeing a person in need.

For example, imagine you see someone along the roadside waving you down for help, so you do the right thing and pull over, only to become a victim of an attempted carjack. I'm acquainted with this scenario because it happened to me.

Incidents like this cause us to second-guess helping others. In the parable of the Good Samaritan, the first two individuals who passed by the injured man may have feared for their lives because of the frequent robberies, and they may have concluded that the wounded man was an ambush. Their concern for their own safety outweighed their compassion for their fellow man. Love grows cold because iniquity abounds, and many will take advantage of those willing to help.

However, these challenges shouldn't deter us from our acts of charity. It's true that when you help others, they might take advantage of you. And you will feel as if someone has tricked you. We must persist and press on. It's crucial to pray for our love to grow and thrive, even in the face of increasing iniquity. We cannot afford to lose one of the most essential aspects of our faith. To paraphrase I Corinthians 13; 'I could do everything perfectly, but if I don't have charity, it profits me nothing.'

ELEVEN: The trifecta of "Knowledge, judgment, wisdom."

This topic is near to my heart. We need people who possess deeper knowledge of God's Word and will use that knowledge to make sound judgments, combining it with wisdom. It's easy to get caught up in this subject, as there's an abundance of references in the Bible emphasizing the importance of these three ideals. Therefore, I'll distill it into a single, overarching thought.

As I've mentioned previously, the world is full of insurmountable problems that could benefit from prayer. However, is there a single prayer that, if answered, could resolve most of these issues? If such a prayer exists, what would it be?

As I recall my childhood in the 1970s, I remember being presented with a range of global issues in elementary school; concerns like acid rain, the ozone layer, the impending ice age, pollution, and who squeezed the Charmin. One of the big concerns was the population explosion and the idea that there were too many people to feed. Interestingly, this debunked concern is resurfacing in the 2020s.

As I grew older, I realized that the reason many of these problems persist is that some of them aren't actual problems. People manufacture problems to manipulate others. However, some problems are so complex and deeply rooted in our sinful human nature that there are no easy fixes.

However, I believe I have found the answer. There is a single prayer, if answered, could resolve a vast majority of the world's problems. The root of many of these problems lies in the lack of knowledge of the Lord. I drew insight from the book of Isaiah, which states. "They shall not hurt nor destroy in all My holy mountain; for the earth shall be full of the knowledge of the Lord, as the waters cover the sea" (Isaiah 11:9).

Consider the profound implication of that statement. If the knowledge of the Lord covered every man, woman, and child, just as the waters cover the sea, violence would cease. If we were to eradicate violence on all levels in our world, wouldn't we solve most of the world's problems? Wars would vanish, and so would domestic violence, child abuse, rape, and robberies. Slavery could finally become a thing of the past. All of this could occur if the knowledge of the Lord poured forth upon His creation.

But many Christians don't read their Bibles daily. People ignore God's wisdom. And we all bear the consequences of this neglect.

"My people are destroyed for lack of knowledge. Because thou hast rejected knowledge, I will also reject thee," (Hosea 4:6)

A.S.K.

Do you grasp the importance of knowledge, judgment, and wisdom that flows from the Word of God? I hope you do.

TWELVE: "That ye may know what is the hope of his calling, and what the riches of the glory of his inheritance in the saints."

We have hope. Hope is the buoy that can keep you afloat when all others are sinking. Through prayer, we should ask God to help us never lose sight of this hope. At the end of life, we can continue to have hope because of the promises of God. He has assured us that eternal life is more magnificent than we can imagine. While I've often shared my imaginative ideas of what heaven might be like, I fully know that even my best attempts will fall significantly short of the actual reality of heaven.

Years ago, I was hiking with my children and a cracker from our snack bag fell to the ground. The cracker disappeared, and my son asked if I had eaten it. I told him I would never tell. Perhaps I ate it, or maybe I tossed it into the bushes. He persisted, repeatedly asking for the answer. In the end, I told him that the only way he would ever find out was when he arrived in heaven.

To this day, we still bring up the mystery of the missing cracker. What happened to the cracker remains my secret, one that I'm taking to the grave. Did I eat a dirt covered cracker? I'll never tell. One day, on the other side, my son will finally uncover the truth. And when that moment arrives, we will share a hearty laugh. What is this? This is hope.

"The Lord taketh pleasure in them that fear Him, in those that hope in His mercy." (Psalm 147:11)

A.S.K.

Health

A.S.K.

7

Health

Health is such a predominant request that a book about prayer would be incomplete without addressing the proverbial 'elephant in the room'.

The Bible encourages us to 'walk in the Spirit' of God, and that our physical 'flesh'—our mortal bodies with its associated needs and desires—are contrary to the 'Spirit'. In a way, they war against each other in a constant battle.

"This I say then: Walk in the Spirit, and ye shall not fulfill the lust of the flesh. For the flesh lusteth against the Spirit, and the Spirit against the flesh; and these are contrary the one to the other, so that ye cannot do the things that ye would." (Galatians 5:16-17)

In the preceding chapter, I detailed how we can pray for one another, with all the topics centered on spiritual concepts. However, the health of our physical bodies remains an ever-present reality. The demands of our physical body command constant attention. I dedicate a significant portion of a typical day to maintaining my physical body. I cannot change this reality.

My body requires eight hours of sleep a day, and to sustain myself, I must engage in work to provide food, clothing and shelter. When you factor in additional daily activities such as grocery shopping, household chores, meal preparation, exercise, personal hygiene, commuting, and errands, the hours slip away, all dedicated to the upkeep of my physical being. After taking care of my physical needs, which often require both thought and action, only a limited amount of time remains to pursue spiritual matters.

It is unsurprising that we prioritize physical health. Poor health disrupts the equilibrium of life and could consume all the hours in a day, as well as affect those around you.

Meanwhile, none of this is surprising to God. In fact, He designed the system and instituted the requirement of work.

"In the sweat of thy face shalt thou eat bread till thou return unto the ground, for out of it wast thou taken; for dust thou art, and unto dust shalt thou return." (Genesis 3:19)

Still, we are without excuse. We cannot ignore the command to 'walk in the Spirit'. Perhaps, instead of viewing your schedule on a day-to-day basis, consider how you spend your time throughout the week. Work and chores may easily consume six days of the week, but there's always the seventh day. God called for a day of rest on the seventh day. If you struggle to fit spiritual pursuits into a hectic daily schedule, then separate yourself for that seventh day to seek God. Attend church, read your Bible for an hour, and then pray. Talk to your friends and family about Biblical topics. Take a media break and put the phone in the drawer.

The phrase 'walk in the Spirit' implies an action. During a hectic week, if you focus your mind on God, and daily Bible reading fills your thoughts, you can properly administer your daily physical tasks while simultaneously walking in the 'Spirit'. Your daily physical tasks don't separate you from your soul; your soul accompanies you, even amid the daily physical grind. While you cannot escape your physical needs, you possess the choice to focus your mind towards the 'Spirit' as you walk through your day.

Think about your daily thoughts. Do you intentionally focus your mind on the spiritual? Do you periodically take brief moments throughout the day to say something to God? Or is your mind focused on watching the clock tick towards quitting time, or contemplating your next meal, or harboring thoughts of revenge against an adversary? Do you utter micro-prayers to God? Do you think about how God's instructions should apply to your behavior?

A.S.K.

In prior chapters, I intentionally made comments on the significant number of prayer requests centered on health. While this might have appeared critical of the typical request, I fully understand the underlying factors that drive these prayers. I won't bore you with the details of my personal health, but I've experienced a wide spectrum of health problems, enduring many episodes marked by enduring and excruciating pain. I know the depths of suffering. If you want stories, then I've got them.

So, what should you do when health problems arise?

Foremost, it's essential to acknowledge that health issues are inevitable. While you are healthy, prepare now. There are spiritual measures you can take now that will influence your future well-being—It's like depositing money in the bank for a rainy day. If you do certain spiritual things now, then you have spiritual credit for use later.

One of these is considering the poor. God's will, documented in the Bible, affirms that if you attend to the needs of the poor, God will help you in your time of sickness.

"Blessed is he that considereth the poor; the Lord will deliver him in time of trouble. The Lord will preserve him and keep him alive, and he shall be blessed upon the earth; and Thou wilt not deliver him unto the will of his enemies. The Lord will strengthen him upon the bed of languishing; Thou wilt turn him on his bed in his sickness." (Psalm 41:1-3)

Who are the poor? Applying financial hardship to the concept of the poor is easy, and if you can help others financially, then you should. But I think you could also consider the poor in health. If you are caring for someone that is in poor health, it monopolizes your time. God sees your service, and I believe that such selfless acts contribute to your spiritual account. Acts of kindness and care for the poor will not go unnoticed by God.

Returning to the initial points from Chapter 1, the groundwork for praying during hard times begins with maintaining a righteous lifestyle. The same principle applies to health. Preparing for your own periods of suffering starts with helping others right now, particularly while you are in good health. Your current daily behavior matters, because hard times will come. Follow God's paths today as part of your preparation for the rough road ahead.

PRACTICAL ADVICE

Having set the stage, the question arises: what is the best way to pray about health? While we should pray for others, health remains a very personal thing. There's an old joke about the difference between major surgery and minor surgery: minor surgery is when it's someone else, and major surgery is when it's you. Health often mirrors this sentiment. While frequently asked to pray for the health of others, the fervor of these prayers rarely matches the intensity reserved for one's own health or the health of someone deeply cherished.

When I was in sales, managers would declare their readiness to assist. But when faced with challenges, the same managers would disappear. It taught me a valuable lesson—with my sales deals or customers, no one cared as deeply as I did. I was the only one with the passion and focus on solving the problems.

I have a role to play in my health. It's up to me to eat right and exercise. I cannot consume copious amounts of cupcakes and then lament a diagnosis of type 2 diabetes. However, there are plenty of health concerns that are beyond my control. In such cases, seeking medical help from a qualified doctor is the course of action.

There are small sects of Christianity that shun medical help in favor of relying solely on prayer. I think this is unwise. Medical knowledge is increasing exponentially, and God is the author of this knowledge. God revealed to the prophet Daniel that human knowledge would increase, particularly as we get closer to the end of the world.

> "But thou, O Daniel, shut up the words and seal the book, even to the time of the end. Many shall run to and fro, and knowledge shall be increased." (Daniel 12:4)

We should not ignore the wealth of medical knowledge—it exists for the benefit of us all. I thank God for the remarkable progress in medicine. Years ago, I experienced acute appendicitis. Without timely medical intervention, I would have died. Similar health scares have arisen, and, without medical intervention, many of these instances could have ended my life.

Yet sometimes medical knowledge fails. When a health issue arises, I schedule an appointment to see a doctor, often remarking to my wife, "I hope they find something." This may seem like an unusual statement, but if I'm not feeling well, something is wrong. The discovery of an issue implies a potential solution and a path to healing. The worst-case scenario is when they can't diagnose the problem and relief of the ailment remains elusive.

When medical knowledge fails, I have a failsafe option to pursue. I know a God who has compassion for me and may intercede on my behalf. Again, some may argue that God should be the first option. I am not dismissing the importance of prayer; in fact, prayer can coexist with seeking medical attention. You can walk and chew gum at the same time as the saying goes.

When I look at the entire Bible, God often revealed Himself and intervened in human affairs when there was no other hope. When a circumstance hit rock bottom, and there was no other remedy, it cleared the way for God to act because only then would it be clear to all involved that God had performed a miracle.

Jesus performed many miracles that healed physical ailments. Jesus had compassion for the multitudes of suffering people. The Bible documents several miracles, emphasizing instances where medical knowledge had reached its limits. Giving sight to the blind, healing leprosy, and restoring the paralyzed are all issues for which medical science had no solution, and God received the glory. Below is a story illustrating one such miracle.

"And Jesus went with him, and many people followed Him and thronged Him. And a certain woman who had an issue of blood twelve years, and had suffered many things under many physicians, and had spent all that she had and was no better, but rather grew worse, when she had heard of Jesus, came up behind Him in the press of the crowd and touched His garment; for she said, 'If I may touch but His clothes, I shall be whole.'
And straightway the fountain of her blood was dried up, and she felt in her body that she was healed of that plague. And Jesus, immediately knowing in Himself that virtue had gone out of Him,

turned about in the press of the crowd and said, 'Who touched My clothes?'

And His disciples said unto Him, 'Thou seest the multitude thronging Thee, and sayest Thou, 'Who touched Me?''

And He looked round about to see her who had done this thing. But the woman, fearing and trembling, knowing what had been done in her, came and fell down before Him and told Him all the truth. And He said unto her, 'Daughter, thy faith hath made thee whole. Go in peace, and be whole of thy plague.'" (Mark 5:24-34)

This woman endured twelve years of suffering and financial ruin. No doctor on earth could help this woman. Rather, they experimented on her, and it appears they only added to her suffering. This woman was at the end of her rope.

Except she had hope. Having heard of Jesus, she actively pursued Him through faith. Acquainted with the stories of Jesus and His miraculous healings, she believed in His power. And she put her belief into action by reaching out to touch Jesus. And it worked. Jesus Himself claimed that her faith served as the conduit for the healing power of God to flow into her physical body.

Now, having read this story, you, like this woman, are aware of God's healing power. If you've been around church or Christians, you likely know that such stories of healing persist—testimonies of God's active intervention in our affairs when we seek Him through faith.

Now, let's assume you've consulted with doctors. Perhaps they cannot find a remedy, or your problem defies current medical knowledge. The Bible offers a recommended path.

"Is any sick among you? Let him call for the elders of the church, and let them pray over him, anointing him with oil in the name of the Lord. And the prayer of faith shall save the sick, and the Lord shall raise him up. And if he has committed sins, they shall be forgiven him. Confess your faults one to another, and pray one for another, that ye may be healed. The effectual fervent prayer of a righteous man availeth much." (James 5:14-16)

A.S.K.

This is a very important path, a narrow path with specific steps to follow. If you are sick, the responsibility falls on you to summon the elders of the church. Much like the woman who sought healing from Jesus, you are required to seek the elders. The initiation of this action hinges on your personal faith.

Do you genuinely believe this will work? If not, you are unlikely to follow this path. If you possess the faith to believe this remedy, you must put faith into action and make the call for the elders.

Upon making the call, the elders are to assemble, praying over you in the name of the Lord and anointing you with oil. Finding suitable oil is straightforward—I have one labeled 'Frankincense & Myrrh', a blend of extra virgin olive oil with fragrance. According to God's written will, the prayer of faith shall save the sick, and the Lord shall raise them up.

If you believe Jesus saves your soul from hell and forgives your sins, I suggest you believe this as well. If medical knowledge has failed you, remember, you still have hope in Jesus.

DO I HAVE ANY PROOF?

By now, you know I experiment with these concepts, often starting with small things to gauge results.

To date, all my medical concerns have fallen within the realm of current medical knowledge, and treatments have proven effective, with one exception—an affliction that might seem inconsequential to others but posed a daily challenge for me. I was really hoping to avoid having to explain this, but I guess a periodic humbling helps keep my ego in check.

Since I was a teenager, my affliction was hemorrhoids. I spoke with doctors frequently, but they only offered over-the-counter symptom treatment options, but no lasting solution. In the grand scheme, this condition represents a minor amount of suffering with no impact on my day-to-day activities. However, I would prefer to be hemorrhoid free.

Given this, I tested out the recommendation written in James 5. After all, why not? What did I have to lose?

Upon deciding to pursue this option, I faced an internal struggle. The challenge was twofold—I needed to approach the elders of the church and divulge my embarrassing affliction. Complicating matters, I attended a church where such practices were not customary. I think it would be fair to say approximately half of the members held a philosophy loosely rooted in deism, dismissing the notion that God intervened in human affairs since the close of the first century. The church had a board, but operated without defined elders, deacons, or even a pastor, as the previous minister had passed away. Men from the congregation took turns filling the pulpit each Sunday while the search for a new minister continued.

I would enter a situation where I aimed to convince a group of men, some of whom doubted any possibility of a miracle, to pray over me and anoint me with oil, hoping for healing from God. Not only would I have to explain my hemorrhoids, but I also faced the significant possibility of being ridiculed. Within myself, my struggle was with humility. My pride was warring against the humility that these steps would require. After all, it would have been easier to do nothing, especially for such a light affliction.

Years before I experimented on myself, I had encouraged a young man with chronic bowel syndrome to follow these steps. He never would. Even with his affliction, he refused to even attempt to follow the Bible's remedy. I often wondered if he hesitated because of pride, unbelief, or a combination of both.

Honestly, humbling myself before this group of men was difficult, but I knew a handful would listen and believe. I attended one of the church's board meetings, where I explained the passage in James 5, detailed my affliction, and outlined my reasonings for requesting their prayers. I scheduled a time for the following Sunday in the church basement and invited them to take part. The next Sunday, seven men showed up.

Having gathered the men, I distributed the oil and provided a few instructions. I asked them to pray silently while placing their hands on my shoulders or head. Once each man completed their prayer, they were to remove their hand. When I no longer felt any hands, we would be done. This process took only a few minutes.

The reason I wanted silent prayer stemmed from a desire to create an environment where the men felt at ease praying directly to God, free from the pressure of crafting an elaborate and impressive prayer. I firmly believe that important prayer needs to be private (spoiler alert—more of this in the next

A.S.K.

chapter). Finally, if this worked, no one would know the content of the individual prayers, and therefore, no one could claim that their specific prayer influenced the outcome. Only God would receive the glory.

A good analogy is an old-fashioned firing squad. In executions, some say that only one bullet was live, and the rest were blanks. The live bullet was randomly and secretly assigned to just one member. The executioners fired the guns simultaneously. No individual knew if they had fired the lethal shot. This relieved them of the mental burden of taking a life.

Similarly, private prayer served a comparable purpose. No single man would know if his prayer alone triggered the outcome, if it was a combination of prayers, or perhaps it was our unified act of faith in believing the Bible and following the prescribed path. God saw our gathering, and he heard our prayers.

I also made it clear to these men that I would not disclose the results, and they should refrain from asking. I'm not sure exactly why I felt this was necessary. My unbelief might have been the root cause. Having already subjected myself to humiliation, I was hesitant to face additional ridicule if the experiment failed. In addition, I had no way of proving that it worked. For obvious reasons, I did not want to take a 'before' and 'after' picture or undergo a physical examination. All involved would naturally meet any results with a healthy dose of skepticism. Which is fine, because we should be skeptical. Liars and lying abounds and there are many con men and charlatans. The answer I needed was for myself—I wasn't attempting to prove anything to them. I wanted to know for myself. And if it worked for me, then I could confidently urge others to follow the prescribed path. I could be a witness to the truth.

By now, you are already aware of the answer. It worked. Later that afternoon, the prime offender no longer seemed to exist. Something I could feel for over three decades now felt different. There was evidence of other small hemorrhoids, but they were insignificant and not causing discomfort.

But that's not the end of the story. Months later, the dreaded itch symptom resurfaced. I thought, "Well, this is no good. The itch voids the entire experiment." I struggled to interpret the results because there seemed to be a healing in one spot, but there was no long-term relief from the itch.

However, a short time later, an idea formed. It occurred to me the problem was sensitivity to chemicals in certain brands of toilet paper, and the symptoms were an allergic reaction. A simple change of toilet paper eliminated the itch. I suffered the same symptoms for many decades, but it wasn't until after I followed the Bible's instructions that the idea of an allergic reaction occurred to me. But where did this idea originate? I think I know…

My winding road to healing reminds me; Who can make straight that which God has made crooked?

When medical knowledge fails or is flailing, we can place our hope in God. However, He requires that you walk a specific path with outlined steps. I suspect that, like me, you will struggle with pride issues if you follow this path. I urge you to push through with faith and seek God.

"Every word of God is pure; He is a shield unto them that put their trust in Him." (Proverbs 30:5)

A.S.K.

A.S.K.

8

Shhh...
it's a secret

A.S.K.

8

Shhh…it's a secret

Privacy forms the bedrock of prayer. While I'm often encouraged to pray aloud at church, I've found public prayer to be quite awkward. The only instances where I feel at ease praying in public are in formal ceremonial settings, such as the conclusion of a sermon. During this moment, I direct the prayer toward the listener, aiming to reinforce the concepts shared during the lesson. Concealed beneath this public prayer lies my genuine request: that the listener will remember God's word and act accordingly. Otherwise, my prayers remain private.

Jesus would pray in private. Jesus consistently sought solitude for prayer. Is it any wonder the disciples had to ask Jesus to teach them to pray?

Why is privacy important? There are several reasons, but the primary one is that Jesus commanded it.

"And when thou prayest, thou shalt not be as the hypocrites are. For they love to pray standing in the synagogues and on the corners of the streets, that they may be seen by men. Verily I say unto you, they have their reward.
But thou, when thou prayest, enter into thy closet, and when thou hast shut thy door, pray to thy Father who is in secret; and thy Father who seeth in secret shall reward thee openly." (Matthew 6:5-6)

I often wonder why Christians ignore such a straightforward command. A youth group leader once told my daughter that if she didn't enjoy praying out loud, maybe she wasn't truly a Christian. This kind of thinking is dreadful and contradicts what the Bible teaches.

Why isn't Jesus' command enough to discourage public prayer? I suppose it's because many churches teach the opposite. I've heard people endorse public prayer as a method to connect with one another. While that might be true, it is not the primary purpose of prayer. There are plenty of other ways to foster connections among people, so I don't think it's a valid reason to override Christ's command.

I initially planned to write extensively about private prayer in relation to spiritual warfare. A vast majority of the prayers documented in the Bible are private. Very few are public, and they are often ceremonial prayers. I have much to say on this topic, but I'll save it for another time. I will briefly mention one thing, as the Bible says:

"For we wrestle not against flesh and blood, but against principalities, against powers, against the rulers of the darkness of this world, against spiritual wickedness in high places." (Ephesians 6:12)

If we consider the battle between good and evil, analogies to physical warfare are appropriate. What would you consider the most important strategic element in warfare? I would submit that encrypted communication is the key to success. If your enemy gains access to your communication network with full visibility, then they can counteract your battle plans, troop movements, logistical supply network, and the dates and times of your attacks.

Private prayer serves as our encrypted communication method in the battle of good versus evil. When you pray privately within yourself, you establish an encrypted channel directly to God. It is impossible to hack or decode this encryption. I believe this provides a significant strategic advantage.

In the Old Testament Law, God instructed the Israelites to follow various commands without always explaining the underlying reasons. For instance, God prohibited the consumption of pigs and shellfish without providing a logical explanation. He emphasized the importance of cleanliness without detailing the reasons. Similarly, God provided extensive instructions on the handling of leprosy, a highly contagious bacterial infection. Centuries later, science has uncovered the reasons behind these commands. Improperly cooked pig or shellfish poses a high risk of various food-borne pathogens. Neglecting personal hygiene increases the risk of fungal and bacterial infections. Failure to follow God's commands regarding leprosy heightens the risk of spreading the infection to others.

When Jesus Christ commands private prayer, He doesn't clarify the reasons, apart from the promise of an open reward from God for those who pray privately. This should be enough information to deter Christians from encouraging public prayer. However, I suspect there are essential underlying reasons for Jesus' command that we may not fully grasp until the afterlife. I highly suggest obedience to God's command. Engage in private prayer. Consider experimenting with eliminating public prayer in your life and observe any changes in your ability to pray or the results you experience.

"And why call ye Me, 'Lord, Lord,' and do not the things which I say?

Whosoever cometh to Me, and heareth My sayings and doeth them, I will show you to whom he is like: He is like a man who built a house and dug deep and laid the foundation on a rock; and when the flood arose, the stream beat vehemently upon that house and could not shake it, for it was founded upon a rock. But he that heareth, and doeth not, is like a man that built a house without a foundation upon the earth, against which the stream beat vehemently, and immediately it fell. And the ruin of that house was great." (Luke 6:46-49)

9

Epilogue

9

Epilogue

There is much more I could write. I could fill page after page, further dissecting the prayers listed in the Bible and showing that they all fit the same pattern. They form the prayer using God's word and include reasoning with the request. I have many personal examples from which to draw. After a while, it would become redundant, and the overall message would get lost. My plea for you, if you've never prayed like this, is to start.

My suggestion is to start small. Pray for specific small things. It's sort of like lifting weights. You don't start with the largest dumbbell, but with the smallest. As God responds to your small prayers, your faith will grow. You will pray more, maybe big prayers, and when God responds, your faith will grow. And don't forget to read your Bible a lot. The Bible propels your thoughts and helps form your prayers. Without the Bible, your attempts at prayer may languish because you don't understand God's will that He's written.

I heard a man on the radio proclaim, "You can't prove God exists!". I disagree on a fundamental level. He's not grasping the full picture. While I can't prove to you that God exists, I can explain all my experiences with prayer and God's reaction. This is evidence that you must consider.

The problem with my testimony is that you know all men are liars, and you don't know me, so I could be lying. My testimony alone can't prove God exists, but it provides you with guideposts to follow if you genuinely want to seek the truth. So, while I can't prove that God exists, I can show you how to prove that God exists to yourself, for yourself. After all, you are the one that needs convincing. I'm already convinced. Whether you believe has no bearing on my future. Taste for yourself and see that God is good. If you embark on the endeavor of truly seeking after Christ and you persist, you are going to get a response from God. I guarantee it. Since God is clever, there's no way of knowing exactly how He's going to reach back to you, or in what timeframe, but when He does, you will know it.

"And ye shall know the truth, and the truth shall make you free." (John 8:32)

I hope I have inspired you to begin your pursuit of God. Forsake your sin, accept Jesus as your savior, read your Bible, and follow its instructions to the best of your ability, including baptism. Start earnestly praying.

Beware, if you embark on the journey, you will face adversity. I've seen it time and again. If you seriously start reading the Bible, it seems hardship will find you. The problems will emerge from the most troublesome spots.

I think the reason is that we have a real spiritual enemy trying to cut down growing plants before they take strong root. Why does God allow this to happen?

I often wonder if perhaps God permits adversity to test our mettle. Will you wilt at the first sign of trouble? Or will you push through with patience and persistence? Adversity produces strength. A tree planted and cultivated in a sheltered enclosure is weak compared to a natural tree. Repeated exposure to storms will forge the strongest trees. It's easy to give up and go home, back to your old ways and habits, to the shelters of a sinful lifestyle. Our natural sinful state might appear to be comforting and safe, but that is the most dangerous place of all. Don't bury your talents in the sand. Take your talents and make something of yourself. It will be hard. Take the adversity and harden your resolve to do good and follow God, no matter the cost. This is a narrow path. This is a straight gate that few can find. I pray you find the open door before it's too late for you.

"And He said unto me, 'It is done! I am Alpha and Omega, the beginning and the end. I will give unto him that is athirst of the

A.S.K.

fountain of the Water of Life freely. He that overcometh shall inherit all things; and I will be his God, and he shall be my son.

But the fearful, and unbelieving, and the abominable, and murderers, and whoremongers, and sorcerers, and idolaters, and all liars, shall have their part in the lake which burneth with fire and brimstone, which is the second death.'" (Revelation 21:6-8)

Index

C

Colossians 1:9-12 107
Colossians 4:3 107

D

Daniel 2:20-23 51
Daniel 9:1-3 52
Daniel 9:22 52
Daniel 12:4 121
Deuteronomy 7:9 52
Deuteronomy 28:15+, ... 52
Deuteronomy 30:1-3 52

E

Ecclesiastes 4:9-11 30
Ecclesiastes 7:13 103
Ephesians 1:16-19 108
Ephesians 6:6-7 20
Ephesians 6:12 131
Ephesians 6:18-19 108
Esther 4:1-3 47
Esther 4:15-16 48
Ezekiel 14:2-3,6 12
Ezra 8:21-23, 31-32 47

G

Galatians 5:16-17 118
Genesis 2:18 31
Genesis 3:19 119
Genesis 9:7 31
Genesis 18:25 6

H

Habakkuk 1:2-4 54
Hebrews 4:13 10
Hebrews 9:2 21
Hebrews 9:27 15
Hebrews 10:27 26
Hosea 4:6 116

I

I Chronicles 4:9-10 11
I Corinthians 7:12-13 63
I Corinthians 13 114
I John 5:13-15 20
I John 5:14 52
I Kings 8:29 52
I Kings 19:4 38
I Kings 21:20-24 43
I Kings 21:25-26 43
I Kings 21:27-29 44
I Peter 5:5 41
I Samuel 5:10-12 82
I Samuel 5:1-5 81
I Samuel 5:6-8 82
I Samuel 5:9 82
I Samuel 6:10-12 84
I Samuel 6:7-8 83
I Samuel 6:9 83
I Samuel 13:5-7,22 85
I Samuel 14:1,6 86
I Samuel 14:11 87
I Samuel 14:12 87
I Samuel 14:13-16 87
I Samuel 14:8-10 86
I Timothy 2:5 15
I Timothy 6:11 8
II Corinthians 6:14 .... 31, 62
II Chronicles 20:1-13 35
II Kings 4:1 34
II Samuel 7:21 52
II Thessalonians 1:11-12 107
II Thessalonians 3:1-2 107
II Timothy 3:14-17 61
II Timothy 3:16-17 8
Isaiah 11:9 115
Isaiah 37:14-20 33
Isaiah 38:1-5 24
Isaiah 59:1-2 13
Isaiah 66:1-2 11

J

James 1:5-7 50
James 4:10 41
James 4:3 22
James 5:14-16 124
James 5:16 7
James 5:16-18 7
Jeremiah 3:25 52
Jeremiah 5:26-31 55
Jeremiah 6:16 64

A.S.K.

Jeremiah 7:19 52
Jeremiah 25:4 52
Jeremiah 29:18 52
Jeremiah 32:27 91
Jeremiah 36:22-24 44
Job 1:1, 4-5 14
John 1:1 28
John 3:15, 18-20 45
John 8:32 135
John 14:6 8
John 16:13 27
Jonah 3:4-10 46
Judges 6:1,6 64
Judges 6:11-13 65
Judges 6:14-17 65
Judges 6:18-22 66
Judges 6:25-27 67
Judges 6:28-31 68
Judges 6:34 69
Judges 6:36-38 71
Judges 6:39-40 71
Judges 7:12-15 73
Judges 7:2 72
Judges 7:9-11 73
Judges 8:28 74

L

Leviticus 22:33 52
Luke 6:46-49 132
Luke 11:1 4
Luke 11:9-10 70
Luke 14:11 41
Luke 23:34 23

M

Mark 4:40 26
Mark 5:24-34 123
Mark 9:23-24 95
Mark 10:27 95
Matthew 4:2 39
Matthew 6:16-18 40
Matthew 6:5-6 130
Matthew 7:12-13 45
Matthew 7:13-14 96
Matthew 7:7-8 1
Matthew 8:26 26
Matthew 10:28 26
Matthew 11:28-30 27
Matthew 13:54-58 100

Matthew 17:14-21 42
Matthew 21:21-22 96

N

Nahum 1:7 11

P

Philippians 1:9 107
Philippians 4:7 25
Proverbs 3:6 62
Proverbs 26:27 110
Proverbs 28:9 12
Proverbs 30:5 127
Proverbs 30:7-9 22
Psalm 1:1 63
Psalm 6:3-4, 6-7, 9 42
Psalm 12:5 104
Psalm 17:6 52
Psalm 34:8 92
Psalm 35:13 49
Psalm 37:25 10
Psalm 37:21 63
Psalm 41:1-3 120
Psalm 55:22 10
Psalm 66:16-20 80
Psalm 66:18 12
Psalm 69:1-4,8,10-13 50
Psalm 71:2 52
Psalm 79:4 52
Psalm 86:5 52
Psalm 94:1-2 6
Psalm 106:6 52
Psalm 115:3 6
Psalm 119:4 52
Psalm 147:11 116

R

Revelation 4:2-6 6
Revelation 20:11 5
Revelation 20:14-15 45
Revelation 21:6-8 136
Revelation 21:8 26
Revelation 22:17 16
Romans 1:9 107
Romans 8:26-28 28
Romans 10:17 75
Romans 13:12-14 9

A.S.K.

"Nebuchadnezzar the king, unto all people, nations, and languages that dwell in all the earth: 'Peace be multiplied unto you.

I thought it good to show the signs and wonders that the High God hath wrought toward me.

How great are His signs! And how mighty are His wonders! His Kingdom is an everlasting kingdom, and His dominion is from generation to generation.'"

Daniel 4:1-3

www.ingramcontent.com/pod-product-compliance
Lightning Source LLC
Chambersburg PA
CBHW060834050426
42453CB00008B/687